MVFOL P.A.R.S. / Y.I.C.
7350 S. 900 E.
MIDVALE, UT 84047

Conducting Group Discussions with Kids

D1019933

Conducting Group Discussions with Kids

Tom Jackson M.Ed.

RED ROCK PUBLISHING

Copyright © 2002

Contents of this book copyrighted 2002 by Tom
Jackson and Red Rock Publishing. All rights
reserved. No part of this publication may be
reproduced, stored in a retrieval system, or trans-
mitted in any form or by any means, electronic,
mechanical, photocopying, recording or otherwise, without the prior written permission of the
author or publisher.

Cover Design: Greg Bitney
Editing: Frank Jackson
Illustrations: Greg Bitney
Page Design: BookMatters
Printing: Data Reproductions

ISBN 0-9664633-6-6

Additional copies of this book and other materials
by Tom Jackson may be ordered from your sup-
plier or from:

Active Learning Center, Inc.
3835 West 800 North
Cedar City UT 84720
(435) 586-7058 between the hours of 7:00 a.m. and
7:00 p.m. Mountain Time
FAX: (435) 586-0185
Toll free: 1-888-588-7078 between the hours of
7:00 a.m. and 7:00 p.m. Mountain Time

Web site: www.activelearning.org
E-mail: staff@activelearning.org

**Have Tom Jackson speak to your organization or
conference. Call toll free for information.
1-888-588-7078**

PRINTED IN THE UNITED STATES OF AMERICA

Contents

About the Author

TOM JACKSON is an expert in the area of active learning. He has four previously published books, **Activities That Teach, More Activities That Teach, Activities That Teach Family Values** and **Still More Activities That Teach**. His professional background includes a Master's Degree in Education from the University of Southern California. He spent 12 years as a high school social studies teacher in southern California. Tom spent the next 13 years as a prevention specialist for a mental health/alcohol and drug center in southwestern Utah. During his time with the state agency, he directed the prevention/education programs for five school districts and the surrounding communities. During this time, he also served as a member of the Utah State Office of Education's Curriculum Committee for Alcohol and Other Drug Education and on the Governor of Utah's Substance Abuse and Anti-Violence Coordinating Council.

In 1996 Tom was chosen as the Chemical Health Educator of the Year for the State of Utah. Then in 1997 he was awarded an Excellence in Outstanding Service to Education Award from the Utah State Board of Education. He has made guest appearances on a variety of radio and television programs as well as having a number of published articles.

Today, Tom Jackson is the director of the Active Learning Center, Inc. which distributes his activity books. He also directs the Active Learning Foundation, a nonprofit organization, which schedules speaking engagements around the country. Tom is a popular conference keynote, breakout and workshop presenter. He also conducts trainings for school districts and other organizations throughout the United States. His presentations have educated and entertained thousands of professionals, parents and youth across the country.

Acknowledgements

While creating this book, I was constantly reminded of friends and colleagues who have helped me discover what works and what doesn't work when leading a discussion. I have been mentored by many of the best! I am also very grateful to the generous people who made suggestions and contributions for this book or have given me ideas to share. I also want to thank the hundreds of kids who have been part of the discussions that I have led. They were the ones who taught me the most and the ones who had to suffer as I honed my processing skills through trial and error. Of course the ones that presented me with the most challenges were my own children, Frank, Brent and Denise. All of them were very skilled debaters when it came to issues such as curfew, choice of friends and other coming of age issues.

Three people were especially helpful in the final draft of this book, Shirley Freytag of Colorado, Mona Johnson of Washington and Lisa Miller of Ohio. They reviewed an early draft of my book and made suggestions that greatly influenced the final product. Each of them are outstanding professionals, do wonderful work with kids and are accomplished discussion leaders. Thanks to my good friend Greg Bitney who created the illustrations and the cover for this book. Without his input, the book would have looked a lot like a dictionary—lots of words and nothing else. My oldest child, Frank, once again had the final say as editor. He has edited all my books and does a wonderful job of keeping me grammatically correct, focused on the message and writing clearly. He says that I have a writing style all my own. I am taking that as a compliment.

My overwhelming thanks goes to my wife, Janet, who has always been the one who keeps everything together. She organizes my speaking schedule, sells the books I write and still has time to be the best wife any man could want, a wonderful mother to our children and the greatest grandmother any grandchild could ever have. Janet, I love you!

As always, I praise God for who He is and what He means in my life.

"Conversation is the laboratory and workshop of the student."

—Ralph Waldo Emerson

1 |||| Introduction

Active learning is a three step educational model with the discussion phase being the third step.

When I was first hired as an alcohol and drug prevention specialist, I would go into classrooms and give presentations about the effects of substances on the body. Since I worked with five school districts and hundreds of teachers, many of them did not know my name. To these people I was just known as the alcohol and drug guy. That was O.K. until I would run into a fourth or fifth grader at the grocery store and they would point me out to their mom or dad as the alcohol and drug guy. You should see how fast those parents could turn their carts around and head the other way. That wasn't too bad, but the real problem was that after I was introduced to a class as being there to talk about alcohol and drugs, many students in the upper grades would roll their eyes, settle back in their seats and proceed to daydream or sleep. It was at that

For learning to start, you have to engage the brain

1

point that I started developing the activities that I have shared with thousands of professionals across the country and I began utilizing what is known as active learning.

As it relates to using activities, active learning involves a three step process. The process begins by engaging the left side of the brain. While we know that the functions of the left and right hemispheres of the brain are not exclusive nor clear cut, research does indicate that the left side of the brain tends to be the more logical or focused side. Characteristics of the left side of the brain include being time oriented, analytical, rational, thinking in a linear fashion, and looking for and selecting an explanation for how things work. The active learning process begins when the instructor stimulates the left side of the brain by giving out information. The instructor may use a variety of formats to convey the information which may include lecture, worksheets, having the students read out of a textbook or any of a dozen other teaching strategies. Once this has been completed, active learning moves to the right side of the brain. The right side of the brain tends to be less ordered in its thinking process. Characteristics of the right side of the brain include seeing the whole picture, being time independent, holistic in its approach to a problem, being able to relate isolated parts of information together and enjoying the experience without spending too much time analyzing what is taking place. Once the activity has been completed, the third and final step moves back to the left side of the brain. This third step involves conducting a discussion. You talk with the students about the activity and how it relates to the topic that you are studying.

This third step of active learning is what this book is all about. My earlier books **Activities That Teach**, **More Activities That Teach**, **Still More Activities That Teach**, and **Activities That Teach Family Values** have chapters relating to how you conduct

BRAIN HEMISPHERE TENDENCIES

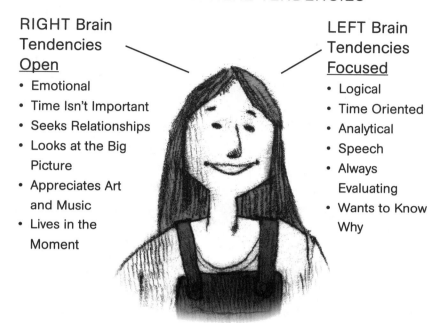

RIGHT Brain
Tendencies
<u>Open</u>

- Emotional
- Time Isn't Important
- Seeks Relationships
- Looks at the Big Picture
- Appreciates Art and Music
- Lives in the Moment

LEFT Brain
Tendencies
<u>Focused</u>

- Logical
- Time Oriented
- Analytical
- Speech
- Always Evaluating
- Wants to Know Why

an activity. However, this book will deal exclusively with the discussion step of the active learning teaching model. There are many words that refer to the act of discussing. Some of them include discussion, processing, reflecting, and debriefing. Even though these words all have a slightly different connotation, I will be using them interchangeably in this book. The purpose of the discussion step is to take what the students experienced during the activity and transfer or apply that information to the teaching objective of the lesson. The focus of this book will be how to make an activity meaningful. This will not be a generic treatise on how to lead a discussion, although many of the same strategies can be applicable, but rather on how to lead a discussion as it relates specifically to activities. An activity without the processing step is fun, but it is really an energizer rather than part of an educational teaching strategy. In order for an activity to be more than just a momentary or transitory event, we must attach meaning to the activity which will help the participants think, feel, and behave in a positive manner in the future.

Even though my books, in one form or another, are called **Activities That Teach,** this is really a misnomer. The majority of the teaching doesn't take place during the activity, but during the discussion phase. We all love to take advantage of teachable moments, but they seldom seem to occur at opportune times. Through the use of my activities, you are able to *create* teachable moments. The activities put you in control of when these moments take place and, through discussion, what can be learned from them.

There is no one correct way to process an activity. The manner in which you proceed will depend upon the size of your group, the time that you have available, the relative importance of the topic, the age of the participants and your teaching objective. Throughout this book you will be able to pick and choose the methods that work well with your groups and adapt the other suggestions to your circumstances. Ignore the ideas that don't fit your needs and embrace the ones that do. That is one of the great characteristics about active learning: it is successful with diverse types of kids and in varying situations. Plus to lead a great discussion, you don't have to be a charismatic, entertaining speaker. You can just be yourself and let the kids do the talking.

Thousands of people from across the country who have attended my workshops have heard me give them two rules about active learning. Both of these rules apply not only to conducting the activities, but also to the discussion time. The first rule is **"Use what works for you and change what doesn't."** Remember, the reason I developed my activities is to give you a chance to improve the life skills and provide personal growth for the kids you work with. When I say life skills I am referring to areas such as communication, goal setting, self-esteem, working together, respect, responsibility, problem solving, controlling emotions, the prevention of substance abuse, etc. For you to make a real impact in these critical areas, you will need to adapt both my activities and processing approach to the specific population you work with. Throughout this book there are numerous strategies for conducting a successful discussion. Every strategy won't work for every group. The trick is to pick and choose from what I offer until you have created your own style that meets your particular needs. Don't look at this book as if it were a mathematical formula which when followed will produce a specific outcome. Think of this book as an old family recipe that has been handed down for generations. Each cook adds a pinch of this and a splash of that to meet the tastes of their individual family. Consider what I have to offer and then mix and match until it works for you!

The second rule is **"Both you and your students will get better the more times you use active learning."** Don't expect miracles! If you are new to leading discussions, then it may take a while for you to feel comfortable in your role. If your students are reluctant at first to join right in, be patient as you try the various steps in this book. Soon you will see your group go through a transformation right before your eyes. Kids love to talk, but you need to give them the proper environment. When I go into a first grade classroom and ask a question, every kid raises their hand with something to say. Their comments aren't always about the subject, but they are all ready to talk at a moment's notice. Go into a high school classroom and ask a question, even one they all know the answer to, and watch how reluctant they are to raise their hands. Part of the magic of active learning is that when you begin using activities to get students engaged and then follow up with a focused discussion that has the right components, you will

The Active Learning Cycle

find that reluctance disappearing. Then you will have the opposite problem: how to find time for everyone to have a chance to contribute. Have fun!!!

| KEY POINTS |

* ⋆ Active learning stimulates both the left and right sides of the brain.

* ⋆ Active learning is a three step process.

* ⋆ Step one consists of giving information.

* ⋆ Step two engages the class in an activity.

* ⋆ Step three uses discussion to relate the activity to the lesson's objective.

* ⋆ Rule one: Use what works for you and change what doesn't.

* ⋆ Rule two: Both you and your students will get better the more times you use active learning.

2 |||| Why Have a Discussion?

Not having time for the discussion after an activity makes as much sense as not having time to eat after cooking a great meal. What would be the point?

"Class, our time is almost up. We won't have a chance today to talk about the activity. If we get a chance, we will pick it up again tomorrow." Unfortunately, a version of this comment is heard all too often when teachers use activities. Things are a little off schedule and time is running short, so the first thing that gets shortened or eliminated is the discussion time after an activity has taken place. The truth is that without the discussion part of the activity, all we are doing is having fun. If you are an educator, working in a classroom or in some other program, then you have been hired to teach kids. Make no mistake about it, learning can be fun. Having fun can certainly be a byproduct of your teaching, but if it is the only product, then you are doing something wrong. Using activities will provide you with teachable moments, but much of that teaching comes during the processing phase of the active learning process. To overlook or cut short the discussion time is to negate much of the effectiveness of using activities as a teaching strategy, and the learning that does take place is likely to be shallow and short-term.

The discussion phase of active learning enables students to take time to think back over the activity and see what can be learned from the experience. This reflection is aided by the teacher guiding the students by asking questions that will allow for critical thinking that can lead to new insights based upon what took place during the activity. Just taking part in an activity is insufficient to ensure that learning has taken place. Some people think that an activity can speak for itself and one will learn by just being a part of an activity. That is the same as believing that a person becomes educated by simply attending school. We need to use activities to help students think in new ways. By analyzing the experience, students can gain understanding and then use this new level of understanding to make practical and meaningful applications to their own lives. Processing transforms the activity into knowledge that is both personally meaningful and useful in promoting personal growth.

Kids today need time to talk and share opinions in a controlled, structured environment. Much of society is formatted to talk at kids, but not with kids. In many classrooms a teacher shares his or her knowledge with their students using passive teaching strategies such as lecture, worksheets or answering questions at the end of the chapter. The media bombards our children and youth with one-way messages all day long that tell them what to think, how to be cool, and what to buy. Computer games leave kids interacting with a machine. Television and videos are the ultimate brain-numbing experience. Being a participant in a discussion gives your students a chance to express their opinions and be heard in a non-threatening format. During a discussion we give kids permission to think and to speak their minds. When kids get together outside of school, they rarely engage in conversation that will lead to personal growth. To be honest, much of the conversation that I hear in the upper grades among students centers on put-downs and sarcasm. A discussion group may be one of the few places where students are listened to and what they say is valued.

Discussion allows the teacher to learn also. When conducting an activity we are looking for certain outcomes. However, during the course of a discussion the students might take off on a tangent. It is at this point that the teacher might learn something new. As the students share what they are thinking, they are actually letting the teacher inside their world. They might relate how they feel during certain situations or how a set of circumstances affects them. When they let their guard down like this, we are privileged to see inside their lives and gain insight into their feelings, insecurities, interests, and thoughts. It is a great honor when a teacher gets to share in these moments of youthful, honest expression.

When students are part of a discussion they:

- learn to take turns speaking

- learn to value other people's opinions

- are exposed to new thoughts

- develop skills in analyzing and evaluating what is being said

- have a chance to clarify and review what they have experienced during the activity

- can have their own opinions validated by hearing from others with the same beliefs

- can be challenged by the teacher or others to defend their opinions

- can measure what they think against what the group is saying

- learn more by discovering their own truths than when information is told to them

- become more bonded as a group by sharing thoughts and opinions

- reflect to the teacher their level of understanding relating to the topic

- learn to listen for meaning and understanding

- become more comfortable with expressing themselves in a group situation

- have a chance to crystallize their own beliefs

- retain more of what is said in a discussion than during a lecture

- have a safe learning environment in which to experiment with different opinions

While students find the activities to be the best part of active learning, I find the discussion time to be the best part. It is here where the activity comes alive and becomes a living, breathing entity. Kids sharing ideas, thoughts and opinions with each other in a safe learning environment is an endorphin producing experience for me. I find the experience to be very rewarding, satisfying, and gratifying. I hope that you find it that way too.

Let me close this chapter with a quote by Arthur W. Chickering and Zelda F. Gamson from their work *New Directions for Teaching and Learning*. "Learning is not a spectator sport. Students do not learn much by just sitting in class listening to teachers, memoriz-

"Learning is not a spectator sport."

ing pre-packaged assignments, and spitting out answers. They must talk about what they are learning, write reflectively about it, relate it to past experiences, and apply it to their daily lives. They must make what they learn part of themselves." This is why we should always include discussion as part of our activities.

| KEY POINTS |

* Just taking part in an activity is insufficient to ensure that learning has taken place.

* We need to stop talking at kids and start talking with kids.

* The discussion allows students to hear the opinions of others and formulate one of their own.

* Communication skills are taught during the discussion.

* Discussion is very important; don't shortchange it.

3 ||| Four Steps to a Great Discussion

When leading a discussion, having a road map makes everything easier.

Active learning is a powerful teaching strategy, but to be effective the discussion must be as well planned as the activity itself. During the discussion phase, you want the students to build connections between previous knowledge and new knowledge using the activity that you just conducted as the beginning point for the discussion. Making these connections is a critical step for students if you want them to apply what they learned during the activity to their daily lives. When the discussion ends, we want the students to be able to answer the question, "What can I do with this information and how can I use it to make my life better?" This chapter will give you a basic outline which will enable your students to make the connection between the activity, the teaching objective, and using the information to improve their lives.

A discussion that follows an activity is different in some respects than other discussions that teachers may have in their classrooms. Rather than the discussion being a general talking session, the activity gives the students a frame of reference. They now have a concrete experience to refer back to and move forward from during the discussion. To effectively conduct a discussion following an activity, I have utilized a four step process. This four step process has been successful with kids across all grade levels whether they are gifted,

The roadmap to a great discussion

average or part of the high risk population. The first three steps of the process are centered around the questions you ask, and the final step is a tool for the teacher or leader to condense what has been discussed and put it into a neat package. The four steps in the outline are **"What," "So What," "Now What"** and **summarization**. Let's take a more extensive look at these four steps.

You have just conducted a great activity. During the activity all of your kids were involved, interested and the energy level was high. However, as soon as you start leading the discussion, those same excited and involved kids become silent as a sphinx. This scenario is all too real for many people who work with children and youth. Whenever I conduct a workshop on processing, one of the most frequently asked questions is, "How can I get my kids to talk?" My initial response is to point out that one of the mistakes I see discussion leaders make is that they start by asking questions that require too much personal risk or reveal too much personal information. When a leader begins a discussion by asking the students to offer an opinion or share a personal experience, they are many times met with a stony silence. Questions that ask for a response about how a person felt emotionally or how this activity relates to things that are happening in their own lives requires a high level of commitment from the students. For example, I observed a teacher who had just completed an activity on honesty. She opened the discussion by asking students to share an experience where they had been caught telling a lie. You can imagine how many students responded to her request.

Discussion—Step One: "What"

When a discussion begins with long periods of silence, the leader feels disheartened and brings the discussion to an end rather quickly. To help prevent this from happening, the first step of the discussion process should be a series of questions called "What" questions. No, this doesn't mean that every question has to start with the word "what." It means that all of the questions relate to what happened during the activity. The "What" questions allow the students to begin talking. The questions are easy enough to answer that everyone will have a response. When you start with easy-to-answer questions that put the student at very little risk when responding, the discussion is off to an energetic start and can build from there. These questions can be open or closed-ended questions. They don't look for any great insights from the students nor are they a major part of the teaching process. However, the "What" questions do serve a valuable purpose. They get the discussion going!

Too many discussion leaders want to quickly get to the heart of the issue and begin exploring the critical answers that will hopefully bring about a change in the lives of their students. Unfortunately, the kids are usually not as motivated to begin this journey as we are. Therefore you need to prime the pump a little to get them engaged. Using "What" questions at the beginning of your discussion will allow this priming to take place.

Discussion—Step Two: "So What"

The second step in the process is to ask "So What" questions. Once again, these are not questions that begin with the words "so what." These are questions which ask what the activity has to do with life issues in the context of your lesson plan. These questions shape the discussion so it moves toward meeting your teaching objective. The questions you ask during this phase of the discussion will be open-ended questions. By definition, open-ended questions are ones that can't be answered with just one word but require some elaboration on the part of the student. Remember that the students aren't discussing the activity without it being a part of a larger lesson plan. You will have already introduced the topic of the day's lesson during the opening left brain phase of the active learning process. They know that the topic of the activity was stress, goal setting, communication, conflict resolution, etc., and therefore have a context in which to place the activity and their comments. From this context, they can take what they experienced during the activity and apply it to what can happen in everyday situations.

The "So What" questions are the heart of the discussion. It is during this portion of the discussion that you will ask for student opinions and have a free-flowing exchange of ideas. The questions you ask will hopefully lead the students to the pro-social concept that you want to teach. If the questions you are asking do not bring about this desired response, then rephrase your questions and keep asking. If the student comments move the discussion in a direction you hadn't planned, simply decide how much time you can allow for off-topic discussion. You can always pull the discussion back on track by asking a question that brings them back to the topic at hand. Don't be too quick to get back on topic. Many times the topics the students want to discuss are important issues to them and may pleasantly surprise you with their relevance. I have found that some of my most interesting discussions have occurred when I have allowed students to explore topics that an activity brought up but weren't in my lesson plan. This second step will probably be the one that will take the most time since many of your questions will call for students to share personal opinions and experiences.

Discussion—Step Three: "Now What"

During the third step you ask "Now What" questions. Here you are asking questions that are designed to ask students for a behavior or attitude change which can make a marked impact on their lives. If the "So What" questions are the heart of the discussion, then the "Now What" questions are the meat of the discussion. Since we use activities as a teaching strategy, there must be a reason as to why we did the activity. Teachers often make the comment to me that their students have a great time doing the activity, but they are not sure that the students learned anything from the activity. It is during this third step that we make sure the teaching objective of the activity comes across loud and clear. The asking of the "Now What" questions creates a teachable moment.

The questions we ask during this part of the discussion are the ones which lead the students to understand how the pro-social attitude or behavior that the lesson is covering can be practically implemented in their lives. This portion of the discussion will not last very long since you are no longer trying to relate the activity to your lesson plan, but rather you are reinforcing the message or messages that you discussed during the "So What" step. We want the students to think about what they can do with this new information. The "Now What" step allows you to discuss how they can use the information that has been gained during the activity and the subsequent discussion and make it a part of their lives. This is where we transfer what they have learned from theory to application. I would recommend that whenever you can, you make this portion of the discussion very concrete before you move on. If the lesson topic is about goal setting, then you should have them come up with a concrete list of steps they can take to help them set or reach their goals. If the lesson is about communication, then during the "Now What" part of the discussion you should create a list of behaviors that will allow for better communication. The more concrete and specific you are with the attitude or behavior changes that you want them to incorporate into their lives, the more likely they will be to integrate those behaviors and skills into action.

The "Now What" phase of your discussion is the most important of the four steps. When writing the questions you will use during the discussion, begin by composing the "Now What" questions first. Ask yourself, "What do I really want my students to know by the end of this discussion?" or "What is the one thing that I want my students to take with them from this lesson?" Once you have the outcome firmly in mind, then it becomes easy to create questions that will get you to that objective. I am reminded of a quote from *Alice's Adventures In Wonderland* which goes, "One day Alice came to a fork in the road and saw a Cheshire cat in the tree. 'Which road do I take?' she asked. His response was a question:

'Where do you want to go?' 'I don't know,' Alice answered. 'Then,' said the cat, 'it doesn't matter'.'" This is why I feel knowing what you will ask during the "Now What" question period is so important even before you begin the activity. By knowing what your teaching objective is, you can structure the activity and the discussion to meet that objective.

Discussion—Step Four: Summarize

During the fourth step you summarize the contents of the discussion. It is your opportunity to remind the students of the important points that were covered. You can emphasize the answers that support your pro-social message and leave out those comments that were off the mark or repetitive. You can also take this opportunity to fill in points that weren't covered during the discussion. The summarization is an opportunity to once again reinforce the objective of your lesson plan and to pull together the ideas that were talked about. My only caution is, do not turn this into a lecture. Make it short and to the point!

I have found two additional items regarding summarization that are significant. Students tend to remember what was said by an authority figure longer than what was said by others and they tend to remember what was said last. Both of these factors are beneficial to you as the leader of the discussion. You are the authority figure and by putting yourself in the position of summarizing, you will be the one that they hear last.

Let's review the four step process.

Step One: During the first step, you use "What" questions to engage the students and get them involved in the discussion.

Step Two: During the second step, the use of "So What" questions allows you to ask for opinions from the students and have them apply what took place during the activity to the topic you are addressing.

Step Three: During the third step, you make your point with "Now What" questions that focus the discussion on specific attitude or behavior changes that could be made considering the information gained during the comments from step two and the activity itself. This third step is used to make the participants think about their own situation and what they could change or strengthen in their lives.

Step Four: The fourth and final step, summarization, is a general summary where you reinforce what was said in steps two and three and apply those comments to your teaching objective.

I have found this four step outline to be simple enough that I can easily use it to be sure that the discussion is on track and meeting my teaching goals.

If you are working with young students, probably second grade and below, then I would suggest that you only use the "What" questions. Their abstract thinking abilities are rather limited, so they may not be able to contribute much to the "So What" and "Now What" questions. As an example, I was leading a discussion with a group of first graders after we had done an activity around the topic of friendship. As I was asking questions, the kids were all sitting on a rug in the front of the classroom and one particular girl kept waving her hand very enthusiastically to respond to my questions. When I called on her, the answer she gave was "My cat had kittens." While I am sure that was a very exciting event in her life, it didn't really fit into our discussion.

However, I was able to keep the discussion moving by responding, "That's great, I am sure you could make some really good friends with the people you give the kittens to."

I use this example to illustrate some of the difficulty you may encounter with very young children. They will be able to answer the "What" questions quite well, but I suggest that unless they are very mature in their thinking processes, you simply explain to them the information that would have been found in the "So What" and "Now What" questions. By choosing this option, you will still cover the important aspects of the activity but will not frustrate your group by asking them questions that are beyond their thinking abilities.

The amount of time you spend on each section of processing questions will of course depend on the group you are working with, the discussion format that you have chosen to use and the difficulty of the concept you are trying to teach. As a general rule, the "What" phase will usually be rather short since its main purpose is to get the discussion going and it utilizes primarily closed-ended questions. You will spend the most time on the "So What" step since it is here that the students are sharing their thoughts and opinions. The "Now What" section shouldn't be too long because you won't be asking too many questions. One or two questions during the "Now What" part of the discussion is sufficient to make your point and drive it home. You shouldn't spend a lot of time summarizing since this is just a retelling of what has already been said. These time suggestions are general guidelines.

Some activities need to be processed more than others. This may occur because of the nature of the topic or because of certain conditions in the group you are working with. If bullying or teasing has been a problem within your group and is now the topic of the discussion, then more time might have to be spent as opposed to a group where you are discussing these topics in a preventative fashion. On the other hand, if you have used an activity that has made the lesson very clear, then you can rush through the four steps rather quickly and use the discussion time to reinforce what they have experienced. If the students you are working with are old hands at processing, then you can even skip the "What" questions and move right into the body of the discussion since they won't need any priming to get them into the discussion.

To help your groups become better at processing activities, I suggest that you explain to them the four step outline and tell them what to expect after the activity is over. To help remind them of the four steps, I put the steps on a poster board and display it in the front of the room so they can see it. By explaining the four step outline and letting them know I will be holding them accountable for it, they will get to the point of making the discussion relevant and successful with very little help from you. They will begin thinking in the four step outline and coming to conclusions by themselves. Let me give you an example. I was leading an eight week course on self-esteem for a fifth grade class. I came to the class one day a week to work on the self-esteem unit. I explained the four step outline to the students on the first week. Each week an activity would be included in my lesson plan followed by a discussion. By the third week, the students were raising their hands while we were still doing the activity and telling me that they knew what the activity was about and how they could use the information in their own lives. They weren't even waiting for the discussion time. They were already thinking in the four step process. I asked them to wait until the activity was over before sharing their opinions with me, but it shows how ingrained the discussion process had already become in their minds.

Here are some examples from teachers who have written to me to share the impact that the active learning process has made on their classes. In these letters you can see the critical role that processing has made in the effectiveness of the activities.

Alison Metz, a social worker at the Indian Creek Middle School in Waterman, Illinois wrote to me about her class and their experience with active learning. "Often simply talking about an issue was not effective due to their limited ability to think abstractly. But give them an activity that they look forward to and watch what happens! By having concrete examples to help them internalize the learning, my group was able to remember the topic from week to week. Best of all, once the topic was illustrated by the activity, the students were more willing to discuss the problems they face and the successes they experience. The activities and the discussion aid in the development of insight and encourage the student to be part of his or her own learning process."

Gail Ramp, the Program Coordinator at the Council on Alcohol and Drug Abuse in Waco, Texas wrote to me with this story. "We have been using your activities for two years in an after school program for junior high aged students. We open with high points and low points each day with time to share important things that have happened to the students and then follow with an activity from one of your books. Within weeks of using the material, I began to see the students processing the activities earlier and earlier in the session and coming up with awesome insights. The following caught me totally off guard. It was a few days before Halloween and as we went around the group for high and low points, it was easy to see that the group was chatty, light hearted and feeling creative. When I shared my low point that my son had wrecked his truck, they began to create a story. I decided to abandon my plan for the day and let them be creative, so each member added a line to the story after I prompted them with 'It was a dark and stormy night . . .' We went around the group of seventeen students three times as they continued to add harrowing details of my son's misadventure. Shortly after completion of the first round, one of the student's began raising his hand excitedly exclaiming that he figured out the point to the lesson. I had to stifle my chuckle (because there was no point; I just made this up) as I asked him to wait until we had finished the story. Upon completion of the story I called on him and asked him what the point to my activity had been. He said that creating this story was similar to using drugs and alcohol in that you never can predict what will happen next and you have no way of knowing the outcome. I was amazed that even though the activity was 'made up,' the students were still operating in 'critical thinking mode.' This could only happen after using the **Activities That Teach** approach to learning."

Penny Judson from Huddleston Elementary School in Lakeville, Minnesota had this to say about an event that happened in her classroom. "For the past six months we have used active learning strategies once a week in our sixth grade inclusion classroom. These activities have taught our students how to get along. This may sound trite until you realize that the students who used to dominate our groups have learned to listen to input from all group members. Our most quiet learning disabled student feels confident enough to tell her group what she thinks they should try. All the students have started to think outside of the box—trying one solution to a problem and, if it doesn't work, trying something else. They are learning that it is O.K. to learn from your mistakes. We find them talking about ideas and planning before they try something else. The debriefing questions at the end of each activity enhance the learning process, ensuring carry over into real life. One time a substitute teacher conducted an activity and upon its completion started to move on without asking any discussion questions. Students asked, 'Hey wait a minute. What was the lesson of this activity?' I feel that active learning has improved my students' approach to problem solving."

As you can see, once your students have become comfortable with the four step outline and the discussion process, magical things begin to happen. When your group reaches this stage, sit back and enjoy—your students will surprise you!

| KEY POINTS |

* **Step one—Ask "What" questions.** These questions refer to what happened during the activity and are used to get the discussion off to a good start.

* **Step two—Ask "So What" questions.** These questions relate the activity back to the topic of the day's lesson.

* **Step three—Ask "Now What" questions.** These questions drive home the lesson's objective by asking about future behavior.

* **Step four—Summarize** the discussion by highlighting points that support the lesson's objective.

* With some younger children you may only be able to ask the "What" questions and then explain the teaching objective.

* Describe the four step outline to the class. This will enable them to be prepared for the discussion.

4 |||| Discussion Formats

Kids like to eat pizza, but even pizza gets boring. Liven up your discussions by adding variety.

When most people think of a discussion, they visualize the teacher standing in front of a group of students, asking questions and listening to the students' responses. While it is true that this picture does reflect what takes place in many discussions, you need to realize that there are many different discussion formats that can be used other than the traditional "teacher ask—one student answer" format. This chapter will list a variety of ways that a discussion can take place. I urge you to use your own creativity to adapt these formats or create new ones for your own use. You can mix and match the various formats to get exactly the results you would like and meet the time constraints that you are working within.

Students enjoy a change of pace, so don't get stuck using only one or two formats repeatedly. You may even use a variety of formats during the same discussion. For

Again?

Large group
format

example, you may choose to use the large group format during the "What" questions and then switch over to buzz groups for the "So What" questions and written comments with a whip around for the "Now What" portion of your discussion. All of the formats will have varying degrees of group interaction and each will give the participants the opportunity to share their thoughts. As you choose which discussion format to use you will have to consider group size, the age of the group, time available for processing, your objective for the activity and the available space where the discussion will take place. Let's take a look at the different types of discussion formats you might use.

Large Group: This is the traditional format where the teacher asks questions of the entire group and one student at a time responds.

This is the easiest format to use if you are just beginning to process activities because most students are already familiar with it. This format also allows you the most control over the discussion and the class.

Advantages: Time efficient and very controlled. The easiest format for someone to use who is just beginning to have discussions with their groups.

Disadvantages: Very few people are involved at any one time which can lead to students not paying attention.

Small Groups: Divide your class into groups of three to five students. Have the groups discuss the activity. Walk around the room and listen to what the various groups are discussing. You can give them one question and have them discuss it until you call time and

Small group
format

then give them a second question, or you can put all of the questions on the board, on an overhead transparency or on a hand out for them to answer in their groups. If you want the class to stay together and work on the same question at the same time, ask one question at a time or use an overhead transparency and reveal each question as you feel the class is ready to move on. For accountability, you can randomly ask one or two groups to share with the rest of the class what was discussed in their group. This reporting out can be done after each discussion question or after a series of questions have been discussed.

Advantages: More people are participating at a time.

Disadvantages: You don't get to hear everything that is being said and you may have a hard time being sure each group stays on task.

Buzz Groups: Divide your class into groups of between three to five students. Have each group select a leader and a recorder. The leader is responsible for keeping the group on task and the recorder takes notes on what the group discusses. Walk around

Buzz group
format

and listen to their discussions. You can use the same steps as found in the "Small Groups" format for asking the questions and how to keep the groups together if you want this to happen. When you have covered all of your questions, have the recorder or a designated spokesperson from each group share the notes that have been taken with the entire group. After the reporting out period has ended, you may want to open up some of the more significant questions that you asked as a large group discussion item. For accountability purposes, when the discussion period is over have the recorder list the names of each person in their group on their notes and pass them in.

Advantages: Lots of people participating, answers shared with everyone and there is a measure of accountability by having the recorder hand in their notes of what was discussed.

Disadvantages: Writing takes more time and therefore fewer issues can be dealt with.

Partners: The more students that you can involve in the discussion time, the more learning that takes place. Have your students pair up with a partner. Once again you can give them a list of questions, have questions on an overhead and reveal them one at a time, or ask questions one at a time for them to discuss between themselves. Walk around and listen to their conversations. Randomly ask pairs to share what they have discussed. If you want to explore an area further, then ask follow-up questions for either the entire group to discuss in a large group format or for them to discuss with their partner.

Partner
format

Advantages: All students are involved and you can easily control the length of the discussion if you have time constraints.

Disadvantages: It is difficult to listen to all the pairs as they discuss, and there is not much sharing with the large group.

Written Answers: Some students do not react well to the pressure of a discussion. They need private time to collect their thoughts and form their answers. Have your class answer in writing a few of your more important questions even before you open up the discussion. Let them keep the paper in front of them and read the answers they have written when called upon. The answers may be revealed to the entire group, in small groups or with only a partner. I have found that students seem to feel more comfortable when they read a prepared answer out loud than when they have to answer extemporaneously. The words on the paper seem to take on a life of their own and the student is just reading what is on the paper. At the conclusion of the discussion, have the students pass their answers in to you with their names on their papers. This will allow you to see what they are thinking and you can comment to some of the students who might normally not make much of a contribution during the discussion time as to what you think of their thoughts. You can then encourage these hesitant students to speak up during subsequent discussions by assuring them that they have some interesting things to share. This works especially well with groups who are just learning how to discuss. I would suggest that you use this format only in the "So What" and "Now What" portions of your discussion time. Ask your "What" questions in a large group format and then proceed to have them give their written answers.

Advantages: The written answers are easier to share and the writing helps those who take longer to formulate an answer. By passing papers in, you have a great deal of accountability.

Disadvantages: They have to be able to write and the process takes longer.

Anonymous Comments: Have your students write down their answers to a few of your more important questions. Have them put their names on the papers and collect them. Remind the students of your question, select a couple of the answers and, without naming the person who wrote the response, read them. Ask students to comment on what you have read. Then go onto the second question and repeat the process. By having the teacher read selected comments, the class may hear from students who might not normally respond during the discussion time. It also disassociates the comment from the person. Comments can be read and discussed while the contributor remains anonymous. This is a good method to try if your class is reluctant to share their opinions in a group setting. I would only use this method for the "So What" and "Now What" questions. Have your "What" questions answered in a large group format and then switch to this format.

Advantages: This format lets timid individuals make a contribution. Writing helps those who take longer to formulate an answer. By passing papers in, you have a great deal of accountability. This could open up discussion around comments that wouldn't normally be made due to students worrying about an adverse audience reaction.

Disadvantages: This approach is time consuming. It also means that the students are not accountable to the group for their comments since they are read by the teacher. The students must be able to write.

Agree   Disagree

Agree-Disagree Continuum: This format requires students to physically commit themselves to a point of view. In your room, assign one wall of the class as the "Strongly Agree" side and the other wall as the "Strongly Disagree" side. Read a statement and tell your students to line up between the walls according to how much they agree or disagree with the statement that you have just read. They can arrange themselves from one side of the room to the other, with those in the middle having opinions that both agree and disagree with the statement you read. Once they have arranged themselves, ask various students to explain why they chose to stand where they did. Start with those who chose to stand on the strongly disagree side of the room, then go to the strongly agree side and finish with those in the middle. Usually those who choose to stand at the strongly disagree spot will have simple-to-state reasons for choosing that position. These people will get the comment time off to a good start. The strongly agree people will also have clear-cut reasons for their choice. I ask those standing in the middle last because their reasons are not as black and white. The middle group's comments usually summarize the statements from both those who strongly agree and those who strongly disagree. Ask at the end if anyone would like to reconsider where they chose to stand and ask them to explain why. Then read a second statement and have them once again choose where to stand.

This is an excellent way to have the entire class participate, even if they all don't get a chance to explain why they chose their particular spot to stand. Simply by having to move from one spot to another, they had to think about their response. If you have students who always remain in the middle no matter what the statement, be sure to call on them and challenge their thinking process.

It is also a good activity to talk about peer pressure and what impact where friends chose to stand had on other students. The most difficult part of this format for the teacher is writing a good statement. It must be controversial enough so some students will agree and others will disagree. Remember that you do not use questions, but rather statements. This format is best used with "So What" questions.

Advantages: Everyone is involved and you can see immediately where the consensus is.

Disadvantages: Presents a lot of risk for some kids since their opinions are so out in the open. You will also have to address the issue of some kids standing where the leaders of the group chose to stand and having no idea why they are standing there. Only a few students are called upon to provide verbal feedback. It is time consuming to move a large group of students after each statement.

Thumbs Up: A less time consuming variation to the Agree-Disagree Continuum format works with a signal to designate how much you agree or disagree with a statement. One good signal makes use of the thumb. You read the statement and then each person in the class agrees by giving the "thumbs-up" sign, disagrees by giving the "thumbs-down" sign and if they are somewhat in the middle then they point their thumb sideways. If you have them close their eyes while determining which way their thumb should point, then you can eliminate some of the peer pressure surrounding their decision. You may call on them to explain their particular choice. This format does not have the same impact as lining up because students can hide their signals or not commit.

Advantages: This method is faster and takes up less room than the Agree-Disagree Continuum. If done with eyes closed, then they can't just mimic the opinions of others.

Disadvantages: They can hide their signal or change it quickly after opening their eyes to match the majority opinion. Not many students are involved in verbal feedback.

Rotating Trios: Divide your group into teams of three. Assign a number to each person in the group. Have one person be number one, another be number two and the third person be number three. Ask a question and have the groups discuss their answers. Warn them that they may be required to report out what was discussed in their group. Have this be a timed discussion. Don't let the time be too long; you want them to be forced to get right in and

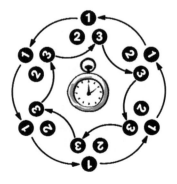

Rotating trios

begin their discussion. Alert them when they have about fifteen seconds left to discuss the question. When time has expired, ask for some of the groups to report out what they discussed. You may assign a different numbered student in each round to report out the groups comments. After getting feedback from the groups, you are ready to rotate. Have all of the number ones move to the group on their right. Have the number threes rotate to the group on their left. This will create new groups each time you rotate. You may rotate after each question or after a series of questions. Walk around during the discussion time to listen to what they discuss.

Advantages: Everyone gets a chance to participate. Groups aren't static so the forming of cliques is not as likely and since best friends aren't together, side conversations are reduced.

Disadvantages: Takes more time to continually move people and you must rearrange the room so rotation can take place.

Whip Around: In this format each individual in the class takes a turn completing the same sentence stem. The answers are short and the students need to respond quickly. The name "Whip Around" comes from the fact that the students answer quickly, one right after the other until you have gone around the entire room. Announce to the class a sentence stem or a sentence with a blank

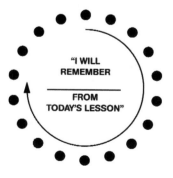

Whip around

to fill in and explain that each person will complete the sentence. Describe in advance the order in which you want the group to answer. Are you going to go by rows, front to back, are you going by table, will you have everyone stand in a circle and go around clockwise? How you do it is not important. What is important is that the class understand the order because once you begin the whip around you don't want any long breaks where you have to explain again who is going next. You may use sentence stems such as "Today I learned. . . ," "I could use what we learned today when I . . . ," "I will remember _____ from today's lesson," etc. Be sure that you give them some "think time" before you start the whip around. Give the students a chance to think about how they will answer and then begin. Move from one person to the next quickly. You will have to decide if you will allow repeat answers or if each person has to give an original answer. This format is best used at the close of an activity or to reinforce one portion of your discussion.

Advantages: This is a good way to get feedback from everyone in an extremely short period of time. Lots of participation in an environment that the teacher can easily control.

Disadvantages: If some people balk and slow down the process, it can become tedious. By the very nature of the format, answers are not in-depth.

Pictures: Have each person draw a picture answering one of your "Now What" questions. The pictures don't have to be artistic renderings, just something that portrays what the student is thinking in response to your question. Divide the class into small groups of three to five and have each person explain their picture and what they were thinking to the other members of the group. Each small group can choose one picture to be shared with the entire class.

Advantages: Uses a skill other than writing or talking to portray a student's thoughts. This process gets a lot of people involved.

Disadvantages: Drawing can sometimes be very time consuming and some participants will balk because they feel their artistic abilities are non-existent.

Floating Panel: Have a group of three or four people sit at the front of the room. You and the rest of the students will ask them questions. Every time a question is asked, each person on the panel will give a short response. After everyone on the panel has responded to the question, the panel rotates. The person on the right end of the panel will leave the panel and sit back down with the rest of the class. Each person on the panel will move over one seat. A new person will be added to the panel taking the vacant

seat on the left end. Have your new panel member waiting to be added to the group so the rotation doesn't take too long. To keep those in the audience from disengaging, the teacher may call on various students to comment on what was just said by a panel member. I find this format to be most effective when I am asking "So What" questions.

Advantages: This can move along very quickly and quite a few people are engaged at any one time. You will be able to hear from all students since everyone will get a turn on the panel.

Disadvantages: The room must be rearranged and those not on the panel must be kept engaged.

Journals or Learning Logs: Having students write in a journal about what they learned after the activity and the discussion have already taken place is helpful in reinforcing the concept that you are teaching. You will probably want to have them write about what they learned during the "Now What" portion of your discussion. In their journal or learning log, they can personalize the information that they heard and make an application which directly relates to their own day-to-day circumstances. It is probably a good idea for these comments to not be shared with other students since personal information may be revealed. If you are going to review the entries, then you should warn everyone ahead of time that you will be collecting the journals and reading them.

Advantages: This format gives each person a chance to personalize the information they learned during the activity and heard during the discussion. If you choose to read the entries, it will allow you to really get to know your students.

Disadvantages: This will add time at the end of your discussion and the students must be able to write.

The following are *not* discussion formats. They are techniques that you can use to enhance the various formats.

Videotape: As an aid for getting a discussion going, videotape the activity the students were involved in. Show the videotape to the class and stop it at strategic points. Ask the class what they saw going on and discuss various segments.

Tokens: This technique helps when you have a few students who dominate the discussions. Give everyone a certain number of tokens or chips. Each time they have a turn during the discussion, they must surrender one of their tokens. When they are out of tokens, they can not say anything else. You may give out more tokens as often you like.

Flying Ball: If your class is having trouble with the concept of only one person speaking at a time, this is a fun technique. The technique emphasizes taking turns when talking and focusing attention on the person who is speaking. Get a small nerf ball or similar object that has enough weight to be thrown, but not enough weight to hurt people. The only person that may talk is the one that is holding the object. The ball is thrown from speaker to speaker and physically shows who has the floor at the time. You can orchestrate this one of two ways. You can have the person receiving the nerf ball throw it back to you after each question or they can be the one who gets to choose the next person to speak. If throwing an object around the room is too stimulating for your class, you may choose to use an object that must be handed or passed from person to person. The rule remains the same; no one may talk unless they are holding the object.

Use this chapter as a starting point to find out which discussion formats are most successful with the groups you work with. In the beginning, practice two or three different formats until you feel comfortable using them. As your comfort level grows, experiment with another discussion format. Soon you will have a whole assortment of discussion formats to choose from and you'll be able to move back and forth between them without even thinking. At that point you will be able to mix and match ideas from each of the different formats to create ones that are uniquely your own. Don't be afraid of trying something new. The worst thing that can happen is that it won't work very well and then you can have a class discussion on why it didn't work!

| KEY POINTS |

* Use a variety of formats to keep your students engaged.

* There are advantages and disadvantages to each type of format. Choose the format that meets the needs of your group.

* Get comfortable using one or two formats before trying a new one.

* Formats may be varied even during the same discussion time.

5 ||| Arranging the Room for a Discussion

It's hard to talk to the back of someone's head.

The arrangement of the room can impact the success of your discussion. Think about the last time you were on a crowded elevator with a group of strangers: everyone stood silently facing the door. Conversation is very difficult to generate when you are not able to look at one another. If you want to generate discussion among your students, the best seating arrangement is one that allows all of the students to look at each other. This position allows them to see each other's facial expressions and make eye contact. This obviously can't easily take place if everyone is sitting in rows. It's hard to comment on what others have said if all you can see is the back of their head. Having people sit in a circle or semi-circle encourages a more free-flowing exchange of ideas. If all you have space for are chairs in rows, then you can at least turn the chairs and have half of the class face the other half. The more people can see each other, the more likely it is that they will talk to each other instead of the teacher being the central figure that all comments must pass through.

It does not take very long for your students to rearrange their chairs into a circle or a square. After practicing moving their chairs a couple of times, most classes can reduce the time and noise associated with this change to a minimum. If the space in your room or the time that you have available won't allow for creating the ideal set-up, then do what you can to facilitate easy person-to-person comments.

To stress the importance of how the participants are seated, try the exercise on the next page.

Where the teacher places himself or herself is another factor which impacts a discussion. If the group is in rows facing the teacher, then the teacher is the focal point of all of the comments. If the students are seated in a circle and the teacher stands at one end, the teacher will still command most of the attention during the discussion. If you want the discussion to flow freely from one student to another, then the teacher should not stand at the front of the room or at one end of the circle. By having the teacher sit in the circle with the students or somewhere else where they are not the center of attention, then the students are more likely to talk to one another. This allows the dialogue to flow from student to student rather than from teacher to student and back to the teacher. Many teachers begin the year with the teacher being the dominant person in the discussion. Then as the class becomes more comfortable with each other and taking part in a discussion, the teacher moves off of center stage and allows the discussion to become more student controlled. The timing of such a move will depend upon the age, maturity and ability level of your students.

| KEY POINTS |

* The easier it is to see each other, the easier it is talk to each other.

* Effective chair arrangement does not have to take very long.

* Where the teacher decides to stand or sit during a discussion may influence the discussion.

A   B   C

| **EXERCISE** | Find a partner and stand with one person behind the other so the front person is looking out into the room and the person behind them is looking at the back of the first person's head. (See illustration A) Once in this position, begin having a conversation about what you both did last weekend. During the conversation, the person in front may not turn their head around, they must keep facing forward. Continue the conversation for about thirty seconds. Have each person switch positions so both of you can feel what it is like when all you talk to are the backs of people's heads. This is how students feel during a discussion when they are in a classroom which is set up in rows. When time has expired, change positions and stand shoulder to shoulder with both of you facing the same direction. (See illustration B) You may not turn your heads; you both must keep facing forward. Now continue your conversation where you left off. When time has expired, change positions once again and stand facing one another. (See illustration C) Complete your conversation in this position. Which of the three positions produced the most pleasant conversation and felt the most natural? This exercise points out why looking at one another during a discussion can make talking with one another easier.

6 ||| The Questions Themselves

| Without good questions, it's hard to have a great discussion. |

Have you ever tried herding cats? You get them going in one direction and then one or two of them will strike out on their own. So you chase after those two and the rest of them begin to scatter. Some people feel that leading a discussion with kids is a lot like herding cats. Keeping them all going in the same direction is not always easy. One of the tools that you have to accomplish this task is the asking of questions. You can steer the discussion by the questions you ask, the speed at which you ask them and the latitude you allow the students to have in exploring their own topics. Used wisely, questions are a powerful tool.

Questions are the driving force of a discussion. What you ask and how you ask it will greatly determine the success of the discussion and whether you reach your teaching objective or not. Therefore the questions you ask are very important. In the four step outline that I use when processing an activity (see chapter three), there are times to use both closed-ended questions and open-ended questions. By definition, a closed-ended question is one which can be answered with one word. Some examples of closed-ended questions would be "How old are you?" "What color is your car?" or "In what city do you live?" Each of these questions can be answered with one word. Open-ended ques-

... like herding cats

tions on the other hand may require a sentence or a paragraph to answer. Let's rephrase the previous closed-ended questions into open-ended questions. "What do you like about being the age that you are right now?" "How would you describe your car?" and "What is there about the city you live in that people really like?"

Some people feel that you should never use closed-ended questions during a discussion. However, I feel that both types of questions have their place. In my four step outline, the "What" questions are usually made up of mostly closed-ended questions. Since this part of the discussion is used to get people involved, I don't need to have each person respond in great detail. I just want to get them to start talking. Later when I shift to the "So What" and the "Now What" questions, then I begin to use open-ended questions that require more detail in the response. I also use closed-ended questions to set up or introduce an open-ended question. For example during the "So What" phase of the discussion I may ask, "Are any two people exactly the same?" This question calls for a one word response and is therefore a closed-ended question. The answer would consist of just one word, "No." The next question I would ask might be "How can people be similar but not the same?" This is an open-ended question that requires an expanded answer. This two step technique, where you start with a closed-ended question and follow it up with an open-ended question, is especially useful with younger children who have trouble thinking abstractly or with groups who have not had much discussion experience.

A discussion encourages learning at more than one level. At the same time the students are participating in the discussion, they are also learning how to ask questions. Asking questions is the beginning of critical thinking, which is the basis for many of the skills needed to deal with the issues that will trouble them as they work towards adulthood and independence. By watching you model the types of questions they need to consider when thinking about an issue, they can learn to be a discerning individual. Outside of the classroom, they can then use what you have modeled for them and transfer their question-asking skills to other areas of their lives.

The first step in asking good questions is knowing what your teaching objective is. You shouldn't be having a discussion just because you have some time to kill. By having a solid grasp of what you want your students to take with them after the activity and the discussion, you are more likely to develop questions that hit the mark. A well-defined objective is an important prerequisite to a good discussion. The questions that you use are intended to help guide the students to see how the activity is relevant to the topic you are teaching.

What is a good question?

- One that begins with the words why, explain, how, what do you think, etc. There are no right or wrong answers to these type of questions, so the students know that there really is something to discuss rather than a specific answer being looked for.

- One that is relevant to your group. World hunger may not spark much discussion, but the food in the school cafeteria may light a fire under your group. Your questions should be age appropriate and related to their geographic and social situation.

- One that has enough latitude in the answer that people can form an opinion and argue for their opinion.

- One that is specific and phrased clearly so the students know what you are asking. Here is a case in point. During a discussion one teacher asked a student, "What are you going to do after school?" The response she received was, "I'm going to McDonald's." She was asking about the student's plans after graduation while the student was answering something entirely different.

- One that is short enough for the students to remember what you are asking.

- One that helps build connections between the activity and your teaching objective.

What is a bad question?

- One that the group does not have enough experience to answer. You wouldn't ask "How do you think nuclear weapons are a deterrent to world war?" to a class of fourth graders.

- One that has an obvious answer. An example of this would be, "Would you rather have your children grow up to be like Mother Theresa or Jack the Ripper?"

- One that is complicated and may have two or more questions asked within the same question. Students who don't understand a question or become confused won't answer.

- A fill-in-the-blank question that has only one right word that you are looking for. This turns a discussion into a guessing or mind-reading game where they try to figure out what you are thinking.

- One that asks for sharing too much personal information.

Sample questions

In chapter three I showed you the four step outline that I use to conduct a discussion after an activity. The basis for the outline are the questions that you ask. Let me give you some examples of questions that can be used in each of the first three steps. These sample questions won't refer to any specific activity, but will be representative of various types of questions that could be asked in each of the steps. I don't expect you to use these exact questions, but hopefully they will be useful as guides when you develop your own questions.

Step one in the outline is the "What" phase of the discussion. Here you are asking questions about what happened during the activity. These are not opinion questions that will reveal an understanding of what took place during the discussion, but rather questions that allow the group to become quickly involved in the discussion. The questions are designed to be easy enough that anyone can answer and not have to worry too much about being right or wrong.

Sample "What" Questions

"What was your team's score?"

"What made round two harder than round one?"

"How much time did your team take to complete the challenge?"

"How easy was it to get the object in and out of your hand?"

"What would have made the activity easier to accomplish?"

"If you were given more time, would the results have been any different?"

"Did you and your partner have a hard time agreeing on your answers?"

"How did your answers compare with answers from other groups?"

"What strategy did your group use?"

"What technique for throwing did you find worked best?"

"How did you feel when using your opposite hand?"

"What role did you like better, giving or receiving the instructions?"

"What question or category did you find easiest to answer?"

"What method did you use to make your guess?"

"Did everyone provide input when your group was creating their plan?"

"Did you figure out the secret to the activity before I revealed it?"

"What was one interesting goal that your partner shared with you?"

"How high did you reach in round one?"

"Did you watch other groups to see what they were doing?"

Step two in the outline is the "So What" phase of the discussion. During this time you are asking questions about what the activity has to do with the topic of your lesson. Remember that in the active learning model you usually begin on the left side of the brain by giving the students an introduction to the lesson. They will likely already know that the lesson is about stress management, decision making, communication, etc. Therefore the students will have a context in which to be answering your questions. "So What" questions will ask them for their opinion. It is during this phase that we are making the transition from the activity to the lesson application. Here are some sample questions that could be used for the "So What" phase of the discussion.

Sample "So What" Questions

"How can we compare this activity to trying to do something while under the influence of alcohol or other drugs?"

"What makes each person unique?"

"Is anyone the best at all things? Explain."

"How does communication affect how much a group can achieve?"

"Should we stop trying to accomplish something just because we aren't number one? Why or why not?"

"What role does concentration play in communication?"

"What are some actions that make people angry?"

"How does gender stereotyping influence what we like and what we do?"

"What areas in our lives do we control by the decisions we make?"

"How does creative thinking help us find a solution to a problem?"

"How does a person's outward appearance impact what we think about them?"

"What role do consequences play in decision making?"

"How is respect gained in the workplace? How is it lost?"

"Is money a measure of success in our society? Explain."

"What are some examples of peer pressure?"

"Do people like to talk about themselves? Why or why not?"

"Why is it harder for us to try something for the first time in front of other people?"

"How does having people with various backgrounds help a community thrive?"

"Describe how you can tell when someone is angry?"

"Can words hurt other people's feelings? Explain."

Before leaving the "So What" phase of the discussion, be sure you have asked enough questions and guided the discussion so that you are within the framework of your lesson plan. If your lesson is about the use of alcohol and other drugs, you don't want the discussion to leave the impression that alcohol and drug use is acceptable. If the discussion is creating an impression that is unacceptable to your lesson plan, ask some additional questions which will allow them to see why their opinions need to be reexamined.

Step three in the outline is the "Now What" phase of the discussion. Here you are asking questions that you hope will lead to attitude or behavior changes. The purpose of these questions is to help you drive home the point of the lesson. When possible, the "Now What" phase should result in concrete behaviors that the students can implement in their lives. Attitude or behavior change comes easier when people know exactly what is expected of them. You should only ask one or two questions during this phase. Pick out the most important part of your lesson and reinforce that point with your "Now What" questions. If you ask your students to remember too much from the experience, you may dilute your teaching objective so much that they may not remember any of it. So focus in on what is crucial and leave the rest of your message for another time. Remember to ask yourself, "What is the one thing that I want my students to take with them from this activity and discussion?" Then you can easily write your "Now What" questions. Don't limit your questions to just ones about how they can improve. Sometimes ask your students to look at how they can help others rather than only concentrating on their own feelings and circumstances. Here are some samples of "Now What" questions.

Sample "Now What" Questions

"Why is comparing ourselves to others the wrong thing to do?"

"How can we improve our communication with others?"

"What are some positive ways to keep your anger under control?"

"How can decisions you make today change your future?"

"Why is gender stereotyping harmful to our society?"

"What behaviors do we see in someone who is showing respect?"

"How can we support others when they try something new?"

"Why is it beneficial to consider a problem from the other person's point of view?"

"How can we help someone feel like they belong?"

"What can an individual do to help to contribute to the success of a group or a team?"

"What are some of the ways that you can say 'No' when asked to try smoking?"

"How does respect for rules and the law help our school and community?"

"What role does personal responsibility play in reaching our goals?"

"How should we treat people who might be different than we are?"

"How can we avoid verbally attacking the person when trying to solve a conflict?"

"What is wrong with changing how we behave just to fit in with the crowd?"

"How can people older than you help you succeed in life?"

"What problems would you have reaching your goals if you used marijuana?"

"What are some things we can do to help us understand someone else's circumstances?"

"If you fail the first time you try something, what can you do to improve your chances of success?"

"How does being on time help you gain the respect of others?"

"How does a 'me first' attitude impact our ability to solve a conflict?"

Be sure that the "Now What" questions do not allow the student's answer to send the discussion back to the "So What" phase. During the "So What" phase you listened to everyone's opinion and came to an understanding. Here is an example of a poor "Now What" question. *"If words can* hurt people, then what should we do before we speak?" The problem with this question is the use of the word "if." The word "if" means that we aren't sure but let's just say we are and proceed under that assumption. However, an "if" allows the students to think that the answers to the "Now What" questions will only be applicable when certain conditions or circumstances are present. The correct wording of this question should be, *"Since we know* words can hurt people, what should we do before we speak?" The way the second question is written assumes that we have already decided in the "So What" phase that words can hurt people. This takes all of the ambiguity out of the question and clearly reinforces the concept that words do hurt people, so now what should we do about it.

Don't be like the archer who when asked how they always hit the bull's eye replied, "Oh it's simple. I shoot first and then draw the circle where I hit."

Should I have a written list of questions that I want to ask during the discussion time? If you are new at leading a discussion, then I would recommend that you have at least a few key questions written down. First of all, this will help you before the activity to focus in on what you are really trying to teach with the activity. I would certainly encourage you to have your "Now What" question in writing. This will ensure that after spending quite a bit of time setting up your teachable moment, you are ready to take advantage of all of that hard work. Don't be like the archer who when asked how they always hit the bull's eye replied, "Oh it's simple. I shoot first and then draw the circle where I hit." Having a couple of key questions for each of the "What," "So What," and "Now What" stages of the discussion will help you keep on task if things begin to get crazy or time becomes short. Don't lock yourself into these predetermined questions. As you watch your group go through the activity you might want to jot down a couple of questions that relate specifically to something that happened during the activity. This helps to personalize the activity and keeps the questions relevant to the group you are working with. If you find a question that worked well, make a note of it and be sure to ask it again with the next group you work with. If you keep such a list, you will soon have a list of "can't miss" questions for each activity you conduct.

If you are working with a group that is experienced at discussing, then you can take a couple of short cuts during the "So What" phase. For these types of groups, the questions I use most regularly are: "What can this activity teach us about the topic we are working on today?" or "Tell me how this activity relates to the topic we are working on today?" Many times the activity itself has been so clear and the kids are so used to making the connections that the kids are ready to jump right in with what they think. Even beginning groups start to get the hang of how to relate the activities back to the lesson topic. Suzanne Beliveau, an eighth grade health educator in Florida, wrote to me with her observation. "I love it when we are in the midst of an activity and I hear the kids say, 'What is the point of this activity?' because they always figure out the answer to this question during our discussion session after the activity. I feel as if I am able to see the lightbulbs turn on in their heads during our discussion time."

One additional question that I have used to be sure that everyone is finished with the discussion is a simple but effective one. I conclude with, "Are there any further thoughts before we move on?" This question gives the group a chance to express any unspoken comments and lets them know that we are transitioning to something else.

Follow-up questions

Sometimes after you have asked your thought provoking question, the discussion can run into some rough spots. This is where you can use follow-up questions to help move the discussion along or to give it a boost. You may want to also use this type of question to help clarify statements, to look at an issue more deeply, to redirect the discussion to another student or to draw someone into the discussion. Let me give you an example of when to use a follow-up question to help clarify a statement. If a student were to use a general statement such as "All politicians are crooks" or "Everyone does it," then you would want to follow this up and find out exactly what they mean. Many times we do a disservice to our students when we allow a general statement to be made without asking them to explain further. Their explanation may be the most meaningful and revealing part of their answer. By asking them to expand or explain further we are able to understand more about what they are actually thinking and the process they used to arrive at their opinion or conclusion.

Here are a few sample questions that can help you expand or further your discussion.

"Can you give us an example . . ."

"What did you mean when you said . . ."

"What makes you believe that?"

"Please explain what you just said."

"What reason do you have to feel that way?"

"What part of the activity do you base your opinion on?"

"Could you expand on that?"

"What other feelings did you feel?"

"Please tell us more about . . ."

"What did you mean by . . . ?"

"What else can you add?"

"Susan, what do you think about John's answer?"

"Jesse, tell us what you think."

"Well, we have heard from Mindy. Greg, what do you think?"

"Thanks Armando. Jessica, what do you think?"

"Brandon, you have said some interesting things. What do others think?"

Questions you could use to complete the lesson

Write on the board or make a chart with the following sentence stems on it:

Today I learned that . . .

Today I re-learned that . . .

Today I noticed that . . .

Today I discovered that . . .

Today I realized that . . .

Use this chart at the end of the discussion. Have the students complete the sentence using one of the listed options along with their thought for the day. If you use these same sentence stems often, then you may want to mount the chart on colored paper, laminate it and hang it in the room.

Asking good questions during the discussion period is a skill that can be learned. After each of your first few discussions, sit down and analyze what worked and what didn't work. Then when leading future discussions you will know what you want to repeat and what you don't want to ask next time. It's true that some people are better at asking questions than others, but everyone can improve their skills by following the guidelines listed in this chapter and learning from past failures and successes.

| KEY POINTS |

* Having a great discussion means asking good questions.

* Both open-ended and closed-ended questions may be used during a discussion.

* Good questions are those which are clear, concise, relevant and age appropriate.

* Bad questions are complicated, ask for too much personal disclosure, or have an obvious answer.

* Writing your questions down before the discussion can help you remember key points you want to cover.

* Follow-up questions can be used to keep the discussion moving and to engage non-participating students.

7 ‖‖‖ The Teacher's Role in a Discussion

What you do and what you don't do is critical to having a successful discussion.

For one semester during college, I was a coxswain for the men's crew team at the University of Southern California. The coxswain is the person who sits at the back of the boat, which in this case was called an eight man shell, and steers by pulling on a couple of ropes which are connected to a small rudder. In addition to steering, the coxswain had the job of keeping the eight rowers in sync with each other so they rowed as a team. The coxswain determined when they would row, where they would row, how fast they would row, and handle the launching and docking process. The only job the rowers had was to follow the commands of the coxswain and row, row, row. It was the docking process that became my undoing.

We practiced in the Los Angeles harbor early in the morning. The salt water was cold and the harbor was somewhat polluted. One foggy morning as we were docking, I was calling out the commands to get the rowers out of the boat. Somehow I got the commands out of order and I asked for them to unlock their oars and then stand up. Now getting out of a crew shell is no small feat since crew members are usually over six feet tall and muscular. Any quick movement on their part will tip the boat over, which is why you unlock the oarlocks after two of them have gotten onto the

Nobody really learns when the teacher's doing all the thinking

dock and can steady the boat. Being tired, they weren't thinking for themselves and just followed my commands. Unfortunately, since I had them unlock the oarlocks before it was the proper time, the boat turned over and all nine of us went for a swim. The point of this story is that I was doing all of the thinking for the team. They were just going through the motions. I have seen too many discussions where the teacher is doing all of the work and the students are just going through the motions. So what is the teacher's role during a discussion?

The teacher or discussion group leader's job is to create an atmosphere where learning can take place. You are there to guide the discussion so the teaching objective is met. A discussion differs from lecture in that you assist the group in discovering what they can learn from the activity rather than simply telling them what they should have learned. In Howard Hendricks' book *Teaching To Change Lives* he states, "If telling was the same as teaching, our kids would be the smartest people on earth." While it's true that telling is a fast way to transmit information, having kids arrive at the same information through discussion will add lasting impact to your lesson.

The teacher's first responsibility is to structure the entire discussion. This starts with determining exactly what the teaching objective is going to be. That must be firmly in the discussion leader's mind before anything else can happen since it will influence the rest of your decisions. If you are using the four step outline that I described in chapter three, then this would be the time for you to write your "Now What" questions. Once you have decided what you want the students to walk out of the room knowing, then you are ready to think about the room set up (see chapter five for more on arranging the room) and where you will stand or sit during the discussion. You will have to decide which format you want to use. Will it be large group, buzz groups, partners or an agree-disagree continuum? (See chapter four for more information on discussion formats.) And then you must develop the questions that you would like to ask. (See chapter six for more on how to write questions.) These steps must be taken before you even begin the class period.

Behaviors for the Discussion Group Leader:

Use good listening skills: You should use appropriate body language and have eye contact with the speaker when you are using a discussion format and you are part of the group, such as during a large group discussion. You also can't be doing other things. I know that a teacher has a lot to do in the classroom and multi-tasking is all too common. However, the discussion time is not when you should be otherwise occupied. I have seen many teachers working on papers, writing on the board, getting other materials out of the cupboard, etc. while students are directing comments to them during the discussion. This really devalues the comments of the student.

Move around during the discussion: I like to occasionally change my position in the room during a large group discussion so people in the back of the room don't feel left out. One trick that I have used to keep the speaker talking loud enough for everyone in the room to hear them is to move away from the speaker so they have to talk louder for me to hear them. This ensures that everyone in the room will be able to hear what is being said. If you move towards the speaker, they have a tendency to speak softer since you are closer to them. If you have divided into one of the small group discussion formats, circulate from group to group and spend a little time with each one so you can get a feeling of what is being said.

Allow time for silence: I know that when you are in front of a group, even a few seconds of silence can seem like a lifetime. However, if you want a well thought out response from your students, you will have to give them some time to think. Silence has its place in a good discussion and should be built into your repertoire of useful techniques. One use of silence is to allow for "think time." This is where you give the students time to think before you even take the first response to your question. Give them a few seconds to gather their thoughts before you begin letting them talk. You might even want to alert your students ahead of time that you will be giving them "think time" before taking responses. This slows down the overly ambitious students from starting to waive their hands as soon as you finish asking the question. The period of time doesn't have to be long; even five seconds will allow your slower students to digest the question and at least begin formulating an answer. The time also allows your quicker students to get past their initial response and think beyond their first impression. A win-win situation all the way around.

Another time for silence is after you ask a specific student a question. Sometimes you will want to hear from a certain individual so you call on them even though they haven't raised their hand. They will need a little "think time" after hearing the question before answering if you want them to give a thoughtful response. If you are asking the class in general to comment on what another student has said, they need the time to internalize the remarks made by that student before they can formulate an intelligent response. Research has also shown that teachers will wait longer for an answer from a student who they perceive to be intelligent and wait less time for a student who they feel is not as bright before jumping in to help the student or asking someone else. Remember, just because no one is talking doesn't mean that no one is thinking. Silence is not only beneficial to the person who has been asked the question, but others are also using the time to put together their thoughts.

Use a neutral response to student comments: Kids have developed many coping skills to make sure they don't look stupid in front of their peers. Rather than joining into the discussion right away, they will lay back and wait for others to make the initial responses. Then when they hear the teacher or discussion leader make a comment such as "Good answer!" "Exactly right!" or "Great!" they will jump right in with answers that mimic or are very close to the ones that the teacher has already indicated are the responses they were looking for. Or you won't get any more responses at all since the students will believe that the "right" answer has already been given so they stop thinking.

The proper response from the teacher after a comment is a neutral one. You can say "O.K.," "Thanks," "Uh-huh" or some other remark that lets the student know that you heard them and understand what they had to say, but haven't passed judgment on the correctness of the response. Now I don't feel that this is a hard and fast rule. There are some instances where a student says something that is so remarkable that you just have to say "Wow!" However, if you continually telegraph your opinion of the answers as they are being given, you will encourage a reluctance for kids to venture forth with an answer before knowing what the teacher is looking for.

Ask clarifying questions: Students love to make all-encompassing comments. The discussion leader needs to ask for clarification to make the student become more specific. For example, a student might say, "School is boring!" or "Teachers are so unfair!" You need to ask the student to give examples or elaborate on what they mean by that statement. Without the elaboration, other students will not be able to intelligently comment because they don't really know what the student is thinking. This also helps the student to understand their own position.

Keep moving toward your teaching objective: When I was a sophomore in high school, I had a math teacher who had fought in World War II. He was in a special forces unit and had a lot of stories to tell. Before class we would stand out in the hall and decide who would ask about the war that day. We could always count on killing the first twenty minutes of math with a war story or two. To this day I know a whole lot more about history than I do about math. It is the teacher's job to be sure the discussion stays on track. And by being on track I mean that you are moving toward your teaching objective.

A reminder though that it is acceptable to follow a line of discussion that is initiated by the students. Some of the most meaningful discussions that I have led have been the result of meeting the students' needs that day. It is important that you allow yourself the flexibility to pursue an area of student interest. However, if this is the rule for your discussions rather than the exception, then you probably aren't meeting your teaching objective very often. Where I live we call this "chasing rabbits" because when you chase a rabbit you are led farther and farther off the main trail without ever knowing where you're going to end up. A good discussion knows where it's going and keeps heading there. If the discussion has gotten off track and you need to bring it back, you can do this by saying something like, "Feels to me like we've gotten away from the lesson," or "Let's not forget our main topic which is anger management." And then ask your next question. You should also move on to the next question when students begin to express similar ideas or stop making relevant points.

Maintain control: The discussion time is no different than any other class time. You should continue to use the same discipline policies during a discussion as you have during any other part of your day. Structure, order and discipline must be the norm. If the discussion breaks down into side conversations, even if they are about the topic, then the class must be pulled back together. If you have divided into small groups for discussion and the groups are talking about topics other than your questions, then you must act. These breakdowns may be an indication that your students aren't ready for too much freedom during the discussion time. You may need to use discussion formats that keep everyone together or ones that allow for greater accountability, such as written comments. When your students have proven they can handle more freedom during the discussions, then experiment with other less structured formats. If individual students are disruptive, then apply the same discipline that you would for any other classroom misbehavior. When going into another teacher's classroom, talk with that teacher ahead of time and encourage them to remain in the class while you are working with their students. They know the students and can help maintain the necessary level of discipline.

Control also means that you are aware of the flow of the discussion. You don't want two or three students to do all of the talking. When you see that only a couple of students are dominating the discussion, make a point of asking others to join in. Use inviting questions to draw out the opinions of others such as, "Now that we have heard from John, what do the rest of you think?" "Monica, what is your reaction to what Jesse had to say?" "Now I want to hear from those who haven't had a chance to talk yet," etc. If this is a continuing problem, then change to a discussion format that divides your class into smaller groups so more people have the opportunity to contribute.

Vary your discussion formats: Kids love to play video games, but they don't have just one. Use chapter four and find a variety of discussion formats that work well for you and your students. Remember that you can even use different discussion formats as you move within the "What, So What, Now What" discussion outline. Match the format to your group, the time available for discussion and your teaching needs at the time.

Don't end small group discussions abruptly: When you are using a large group discussion format, letting people know how much longer you will be discussing is not important. However, when you divide into small groups, have people with a partner or everyone in triads, then how long they have to talk does become an issue. Let's say that you have just given them a question to discuss in their small group. I recommend that you announce a time limit before they even start to discuss as to how long they will have to talk about that question in their group. Don't give them very long. The amount of time you give them will depend on the age of the students and the complexity of the question. With most age groups, a standard type question can be answered in about sixty seconds to two minutes. By setting a short amount of time you give a sense of urgency to the discussion. They have to get right to the heart of the matter rather than just nibbling around the edges. You can adjust the amount of time while they are talking if the group sounds like they are still going strong. It is hard for a group to immediately cut off the discussion when you call time. To avoid the abrupt ending, give them a warning when half their time is gone and again when they have ten to fifteen seconds left.

Let the students do the discussing: The discussion time should not be taken over by the teacher to give a mini-lecture. This is the time to hear what the students are thinking. You may ask clarifying questions to draw out more of their thinking, but you don't want to do their thinking for them. Your job is to set up the discussion and then become the guide. Your turn will come at the end of the discussion when you summarize what has been said. That is your time to talk. This doesn't mean that you have to be a silent observer during the discussion. The questions you ask will guide the students and you may need to gently correct any inaccuracies that come up during the discussion that would color the outcome. However, if you routinely take over the discussions, your students will realize they don't have to put on their thinking caps because if they wait long enough the teacher will bail them out.

Use discretion concerning comments from students: This suggestion is directed to the general classroom teacher or after school program leader. If you are a counselor or mental health professional who uses activities to get your kids to discuss personal issues, then you can ignore this caution. However, for the rest of us who are using activities to teach life skills in a general setting, we don't want to cross the line and allow the discussions to become too personal. I have had students want to talk about alcoholic parents, abusive family members, a friend's suicide, past history of drug use, etc. during a general classroom discussion. I believe that unless the teacher is in a very unique teaching setting, you should avoid letting these types of stories go too far. Most of us are not therapists and counseling is not our area of expertise. Teaching is what we do best. A teacher's training is not in the area of what to do when personal problems arise nor how to comfort a child after they have revealed personal information. What happens is that wounds are opened up, the bell rings and the kids all leave the room. Where does that leave a child who has opened themselves up?

Activities leave plenty to talk about without dealing with issues that should be handled by a professional in that field. When a student begins to reveal too much, I would suggest that you say something like, "Michael, why don't you save the rest of that story for after class and share it with me?" or "Caleb, hold that thought and let's continue when you and I have some time to talk." Then ask them to stay after class and continue their story. After hearing what they have to say, you may want or be required (depending on the topic disclosed and the laws in your state) to refer them to someone who does have the expertise to help. This is a fine line to walk since you want the students to be open and honest about what they are thinking. However, you don't want your discussions to turn into a contest to see who can tell the worst horror stories or a forum for revealing situations that can't be dealt with in an open classroom setting. A better alternative is to carefully listen to the students and always offer anyone the opportunity to meet with you privately if they would like to talk. For some kids, a teacher is the only responsible adult they come in contact with in their lives. Be willing to help, but choose the correct forum.

Evaluate how the discussion went: After the discussion, take a few minutes to reflect back and analyze how you did. Here are some of the questions you might consider:

Did the discussion format(s) that I used keep the class engaged?

Were my questions ones that invited discussion?

Did I use silence appropriately during the discussion?

Did the students walk out of my class with my teaching objective firmly in their minds?

What worked best for me?

What should I change the next time I lead a discussion?

What the teacher or group leader does during a discussion is not the only factor that will determine how successful a discussion is, but I believe it is the single most important factor. There are many variables that will have an influence on the discussion such as time of day, day of the week, the mood of the school that day, the weather, etc. I realize you have no control over these, but you can control what you do. Your role in the discussion is critical. Prepare yourself by making the behaviors in this chapter a part of your teaching techniques.

| KEY POINTS |

* The teacher sets the structure and the tone of a discussion.

* Listening skills, movement, allowing for silence, neutral responses and clarifying questions are all useful tools for the good discussion leader.

* Maintain control and keep the discussion on track.

* Allow students to explore off-topic issues, within reason.

* Teachers should not turn the discussion into a lecture.

* While you want open and honest discussion, monitor how much students disclose about their personal lives.

8 ||| Student Behavior During a Discussion

Discussion skills—they must be taught.

Just because kids know how to talk, it doesn't mean that they know how to discuss. Too many times we assume that our students know something and then become frustrated when they don't. Sure, they have learned some discussion skills over the years through trial and error, but is that the best way to acquire new skills? Just imagine the chaos that erupts the first day of kindergarten after the teacher asks a question. Everyone wants to talk at once! The teacher must stop and explain that people must raise their hand and wait to be called upon before they speak. If they don't, we won't be able to hear what they have to say. But taking turns during a discussion is only one of many skills that need to be learned.

During lunch at a conference in Ohio, I left the convention center and headed down the sidewalk at a brisk pace. The noon break was not very long and I had to hurry if I was going to eat a hamburger at Wendy's and get back before I was to present again. As I was hurrying down the wide sidewalk, I looked up and noticed another man who was also walking at a fast pace towards me. Our paths were such that if we continued walking, we would crash into each other. However, when we were about ten feet apart from each other we both moved to our right and we passed each other without incident. How did we know which way to go? It probably dates back to when each of us took Driver's Education in high school. In that class we were taught to stay to the right. I often wonder what would have happened if he was from London where they drive on the left. Would we have crashed? The point is that we were taught what to do in just such a situation. How to behave during a discussion is not something that is genetically passed down from one generation to the next. We need to teach our students

"Excuse me! I have a few comments about this whole 'life' thing."

Discussion skills: kids aren't born with them

what behaviors are expected from them during a discussion. If time permits, it would be beneficial to ask the students to help identify what behaviors are appropriate during a discussion and which ones aren't.

Student Listening and Participation Guidelines

Listen for meaning. Many times people just listen to the words that are being spoken. Instead, we need to listen for the meaning and the feelings that are behind the words that are being said. If you aren't sure that you completely understood what the speaker was saying, stop them and ask for clarification. You can easily evaluate yourself on how well you have listened. When a speaker is finished ask yourself, "Can I correctly rephrase what I just heard?" If you can't, then you really didn't listen!

Have eye contact and positive body language. Looking at the person when they speak makes them feel like you are connecting with what they say. When you add positive body language, such as nodding your head at appropriate intervals, leaning forward in your chair rather than lounging, having your arms open rather than crossed, and using positive facial expressions are all behaviors which show that you care about what is being said rather than just watching someone else talk or waiting for your turn.

Keep an open mind. You need to set aside your opinions long enough to consider what the speaker is saying. Some barriers to this type of listening are hearing only what we want to hear, our dislike for the person speaking, jumping to conclusions after just a few words have been spoken, or dismissing the opinion being expressed because it is too different from what we already think.

Have respect for each other. Only one person can be understood at a time, so only one person should be speaking at a time. Sarcasm, ridicule and put-downs, even when funny, have no place in a discussion. These kinds of comments discourage people from wanting to take part in the discussion. A student who has been publicly humiliated will try to become invisible. We want to develop an atmosphere that says "all comments are welcome here." Be sure that when exchanging ideas the comments focus on the opinions not the person. Personal attacks, such as name-calling, inhibit rather than encourage dialogue. Remember that there is a human being with feelings and emotions behind every comment.

Discussion Personalities

In many discussion groups there are certain types of personalities that may emerge which can inhibit a discussion. Part of learning how to be a contributing and positive part of a discussion is to see yourself as others see you and make adjustments when necessary. By sharing with your class the various types of inhibiting personalities and their characteristics, you might be able to discourage your students from assuming these roles, or at least mitigate their impact on your discussion.

The Know It All: This person is usually the first to speak and feels that after they have given their opinion, the discussion is basically over. To counter this type of strong personality, you as the discussion leader may want to point out areas where they need to consider other alternatives or you may challenge them on their beliefs. If you allow them to make their statements without a challenge, then the rest of the group will be intimidated and the discussion will end.

The Dominator: "My way or the highway" may be the defining nature of this discussion personality. They can often be described as having a false sense of superiority. They usually talk long, loud and in extremes on any issue you bring up. They have a tendency to interrupt others and when all else fails, resort to name calling. They will quickly squelch any feeling of give-and-take in the group. You might want to take them aside privately and ask them to practice their listening skills rather than talking during the next discussion. Putting a muzzle on them for one session and then privately asking them about the experience may be enough to change their behavior. If they persist, you may want to use a discussion format that doesn't allow them to exhibit these behaviors. Take a look at chapter four and choose a format that doesn't allow them to create problems for the group such as one of the writing formats or the use of tokens. Keep working with them individually regarding their actions so they eventually do learn how to listen to other opinions during a group discussion.

The Pleaser: At first you may wonder why this discussion personality would be a barrier to open discussion. They are usually one of the first people to volunteer when you ask a question. The problem is that their answer is not necessarily well thought out or even what the person answering the question really believes. The pleaser will attempt to read the teacher's mind and give the answer that they think the teacher wants to hear. The rest of the class will come to depend on this person. They will let him or her answer as many questions as the teacher will allow while they sit back and remain disengaged. Since we want to get everyone involved, be sure you don't allow one person to derail the discussion by simply mouthing a response that makes the teacher happy and on the surface sounds good. If you would like, you can play Devil's Advocate with this type of personality and require them to give reasons to support their answers.

The Diplomat: This personality loves it when everyone gets along. Disagreements and strong opinions tend to upset them. They will work towards getting everyone to agree with each other. If allowed to flourish, they will hurt your discussion by taking the fire out of

The diplomat

it and leaving just the empty shell of compromise. A good discussion may have two sides with valid arguments for both sides. Explain to the group that not everyone will feel exactly the same about each of the topics you discuss and that this is O.K. The group doesn't always have to have complete consensus at the end of your discussions, just enough agreement that you can summarize the comments that were made and end up reaching your teaching objective.

The Energizer Bunny: This person just keeps on talking and talking and talking. They aren't necessarily worried about making sense or even making a point, they just want to be the center of attention. An easy defense against this person continuing their filibuster is to gently interrupt them and say "Thanks, John. Who else has a comment to make?"

The Comic: Humor has its place in a discussion, but this person takes it to an extreme. At times funny comments can be beneficial. They may provide some comic relief when the discussion becomes too intense or may bring a group to life. However, there is such a thing as too much of a good thing. If your discussion becomes a setting for someone to practice their standup comic routine, then you must intervene. This is especially true if the humor is directed at individuals either because of something they said or what took place during the activity. Your students will not want to participate in the activities or vocalize their thoughts if their contributions are simply fodder for the next joke. You will want to intervene immediately if the comments are hurtful towards someone. You can make a general statement to the class that no one has the right to verbally abuse another individual even if it is done in a humorous manner. If this problem continues, then speak privately with the offenders and explain to them that you will not tolerate humor that comes at the expense of people's feelings.

The Clam: This is the silent type. They seem to be disengaged during the discussion. There may be a reason for their behavior. If it is just an every once in a while occurrence, then don't worry about it; kids live with a lot on their minds these days. However, if it is a persistent behavior, then you may want to address it. First of all, realize that silence doesn't necessarily mean not paying attention or being disengaged. Watch their body language and use that to determine if they are following the discussion or not. Another tip may be to direct a question to them regarding what someone else has said. This will let you know if they were listening or not. The problem this personality brings to the discussion is obvious; if you have too many of these types then you don't have a discussion—just a lot of silence. I suggest that you approach these individuals privately and ask them what their response would have been to some of the questions that you asked. After listening to their opinions, encourage them to speak up in class because what they have to say will make a contribution to the group.

The Debater: No matter what is said, this person disagrees with it. They will argue the other side of any topic. It's true that this personality type will add some fire to your discussion, but if this is all they do, then your group will eventually tire of them and just stop talking. When someone argues just for the sake of arguing, then the discussion process is brought to a standstill because each and every point is debated ad nauseam without any progress being made. It is best to call a halt and move on when the discussion begins to cover ground that has already been covered.

Teaching your students which behaviors they shouldn't engage in during a discussion means that you are also teaching them what the appropriate behaviors are. Each of these discussion personalities can have a negative impact on your group and limit the success of your discussions. If these personality types become a problem within your class, take time to point out the problems that each personality brings to the discussion. By dealing with this issue up front, you may save yourself a great deal of time down the road. If you would like to demonstrate what can happen when these types of behaviors occur, try this exercise with your class.

| **EXERCISE** | Assign each of the discussion personalities that I have described to one or more of your students. Then hold a discussion around any topic you wish, but have the students who have been assigned the various personalities act like this type of person. If you wish, you may also assign a few people to respond "I don't know" to any question you ask. (See more on this in chapter ten) The resulting discussion disaster will clearly make your point.

When teaching your students appropriate and inappropriate discussion behaviors, you are really teaching them one of the secrets of good communication. That secret is showing respect and understanding for others through your attitude and behavior. Once they learn to apply these skills, their lives will be more rewarding in many areas.

| KEY POINTS |

* Students need to be taught good discussion skills.

* Appropriate listening skills and respect for others will help students beyond the classroom.

* Negative discussion personality types create a hostile discussion environment.

9 ||| Getting Kids to Talk

When you've tried everything else, give these strategies a try.

I went into a first grade classroom and asked the kids a series of questions. I asked "How many of you can ride an elephant?" "How many of you can run a marathon?" and "How many of you could swim across the ocean?" In this class of about twenty-five first graders, every hand went up after every question. And they didn't just raise their hands, they waved them enthusiastically. In due course I found out that many of them didn't know what a marathon was nor had ever seen the ocean, but they were willing and anxious to raise their hand. I have asked similar types of questions of high school groups. Not only do they not enthusiastically wave their hands, they don't raise them at all. Somehow as students move through the grades, they lose that zeal for life and it is reflected in their lack of willingness to share their thoughts and ideas. Since the primary purpose of a discussion is to talk, you can see a built in problem. We see the kindergarten teacher who has to limit the number of kids that get to talk and the high school teacher who feels like a dentist pulling teeth to get his or her students to participate in a discussion.

Active learning has a built in advantage over other teaching strategies when it comes to getting kids to talk. By using an activity, we give the students something safe to talk about. Leslie

Somehow as students move through the grades, they lose that zeal for life and it is reflected in their lack of willingness to share their thoughts and ideas.

Perruquet teaches an academic success class at a high school in Monroe, North Carolina. She wrote to me with this comment. "Several of my students are reluctant to answer questions in class. But after participating in your activities, they are more comfortable in sharing their responses to the questions in classroom discussions." By conducting an activity first and then using the "What, So What and Now What" discussion outline, you create an atmosphere that encourages student participation.

Before we spend time talking about what you can do to help kids become involved in the discussion process, let's take a look at some of the barriers that may make students hesitant to participate.

1. The topic or issue is too broad or not relevant.

2. You start your discussion by asking questions which are too personal.

3. The questions are confusing.

4. The room is set up poorly for a discussion to take place.

5. The students have very little background on the topic you wish to discuss.

6. The age spread in the discussion group is too wide.

7. Certain people always dominate the discussion.

8. The teacher is just looking for the "right" answers.

9. The answer to the question is so obvious that there really isn't anything to discuss.

10. The students are afraid of being criticized or laughed at.

Some of the barriers from this list have been dealt with in other chapters. You should use the following techniques in conjunction with the ideas and techniques found in those chapters. The rest of this chapter will look at some additional techniques you can use to motivate your students to share their ideas and be active discussion participants.

Create a psychologically safe environment

Abraham Maslow said, "Human beings have within them two sets of forces or needs—one that strives for growth and one that clings to safety. A person who must choose between these two needs will choose safety over growth. The need to feel secure must be met before the need to reach out, take risks, and explore can be entertained. Growth takes place in little steps and each step forward is made possible by the feeling of being safe, of operating out into the unknown from a safe home port." Therefore, if you want kids to talk about things that are really meaningful in their lives, you must provide a safe environment for them to do so. I have found that kids will go to extremes to avoid being embarrassed. If they think people are going to laugh at them or think they are stupid, then they will just take the safe road and not say anything at all. You must establish rules that eliminate sarcastic comments, put-downs, criticism of individuals or humor at the expense of someone's feelings. This mandate will take close monitoring on your part, but the results are worth it. When you do hear a violation of the rule, stop the class and remind them that such talk is inappropriate and will not be tolerated. If an individual continues to engage in this type of behavior, then either talk with them privately or enforce compliance through the use of your normal methods of classroom behavior management.

Encourage people directly

This consists of simply asking people to join in the discussion. Sometimes you will have students who are just unwilling to take the step of raising their hand. However, when you ask a student to respond, the pressure is not as great since you, as the authority figure, have requested them to participate. You may be able to draw them into the discussion by directing a question to them or asking them to react to what someone else has said. Examples of this might be, "John, you look like you are thinking hard. What can you contribute?" "Maria, you seem to be having a reaction to Mike's statement. Please share with us." or "Barbara, what can you add to this topic?" You can continue to encourage them this way until they become ready to participate without your prompting.

Even though I am not an advocate of quantifying student comments by saying "Great Job" or "That was very good," (see chapter seven regarding neutral responses) I do make an exception if I have a student who is hesitant to participate in the discussion. When they make a comment, I sometimes affirm their contribution as a means of encouraging them to express themselves more often.

Encourage people indirectly

There are two indirect methods that I will suggest. The first is to simply use a discussion format that allows students to feel more comfortable. Consider formats (see chapter four) that consist of sharing with a partner or dividing into small groups. Written answers can also help reluctant individuals contribute. After they have completed their written answers, you can have open sharing. For some reason, students feel less threatened when sharing ideas that they have already written down.

A second indirect method is to talk with them privately. You can take a quiet student aside after the discussion and ask them what they thought about the activity. After listening to them, affirm that their answers have merit and you would like to hear from them during the class discussion so others could benefit from what they are thinking. Hopefully this will build their confidence to a level where they feel comfortable enough to contribute in the future. Another avenue is to build a stronger personal relationship with students who are reluctant to comment. Even brief, one-on-one encounters can sometimes be enough to encourage students to speak up in class. This may take the form of asking about how their weekend went or discussing an upcoming event they are going to be involved in. When students get the message that you are interested in them as individuals, rather then just names on a roll sheet, they want to show their appreciation by being a part of the classroom process.

Use feeling words

Here is a method that has been a great way to generate input from kids who normally say very little. The technique works like this.

Take pieces of tag board or 4 × 6 note cards and print feeling words on them with a marker. Only print one feeling word per card. Then after an activity has been completed, spread these cards on the floor or a table. Direct the students to look over the words and choose the card that most closely explains the feelings they experienced during the activity. You might want to have duplicates of certain feelings if you think that many students might have shared that same feeling. However, don't let them get stuck on just one feeling. They will have experienced more than one feeling during the activity, so direct them to choose a card that is left which most closely describes a feeling they had. If you have a small enough group or there are a lot of feeling cards left after they all have made their first choice, offer to let them make an additional selection.

Once they have chosen their cards, have the students sit down. When everyone has been seated, have them share their cards with the group. During the sharing time, have each person explain why they chose that particular feeling card and what happened during the activity to make them feel that way. This can be done in a large group or you can break them into smaller groups to share. Remember that you want to have as many students engaged in the discussion as possible. Smaller groups will allow this to happen. If you have broken into smaller groups, then as part of closure you may then have some people share again with the entire group.

I have found that by using the cards, kids are more willing to share. They use the card as a crutch that allows them to hide behind the paper like it is the paper talking rather than them. By choosing the card, they have already made their decision on what they want to talk about. When it is their turn to talk, they feel quite free explaining why they chose the card rather than being stuck on explaining the feeling. I realize that choosing a feeling card as opposed to choosing a feeling out of their head may seem like a small difference to you, but believe me when I say it makes a real difference to kids. This is an especially good tool when dealing with younger kids who have trouble verbalizing or older youth that don't discuss easily.

Here is a list of feeling words that you can start with. Add to this list words that are common with your kids. My own collection of feeling cards includes over one hundred words.

excited	silly	surprised
angry	bored	disappointed
determined	worried	sad
proud	lonely	scared
embarrassed	happy	frustrated
important	challenged	picked on
anxious	organized	overwhelmed
effective	powerful	infuriated
restless	confused	exhausted
intelligent	defeated	eager
pressured	ignored	terrible
mixed up	cheerful	relaxed
emotional	flexible	calm
stupid	helpless	disagreeable
hurt	bitter	nervous
irritated	tense	threatened
lazy	bossy	quarrelsome

All talk

This method helps with two problems at once. It slows down the person who is always talking and forces those who don't normally talk to contribute. This works best in small groups of three to five. Have each group get in a circle. Ask everyone to put their thumbs up. Then ask a question and give the group a certain period of time to answer. The group members may respond in any order they wish, they do not need to go around in a circle. However, once a person has talked they must put their thumb down. When all the thumbs in the group are down, indicating that everyone has provided a response, then the thumbs go back up and the process starts again. This continues until you call time. You may then continue with another question or ask for feedback from the groups regarding what they talked about.

This is your lucky day

This technique works best when you are using a large group format. First you must assign a way to identify each student in your class. To identify your students you can assign each of them a number, pass out playing cards to everyone, or put all of their names in a hat. Then after you ask a question, you will randomly draw a number, card or name and that person is the lucky person that gets to answer. More than one name may be drawn to answer each question or to comment on the answer that someone else has just given.

Call on me!

Most students like to raise their hand in response to a question. The risk to them comes when you call on them and actually expect them to give an answer. This technique allows for everyone to raise their hand, yet with very little risk. Tell your students that after you ask a question, you want everyone to raise their hand. However, when they raise their hand they need to indicate how sure they are that they want you to call on them. They may let you know by how many fingers they hold up. If they hold up one finger, it means that they really want to be called on. If they raise two fingers, it means that they want to be called on but they would rather wait until some other people have responded first. If they hold up three fingers it means that they don't have anything to contribute at this time, but check back later. To use this technique, have them raise their hands after you first ask the question and then have them raise their hands again after the first comment so you can hear more opinions. Keep repeating the process as needed. They can change their finger indicator each time they are asked to raise their hand. Some of them will not have anything to say at first, but they may want to comment after they have heard some of the other responses.

Allow students to talk about the experiences of others

How you ask a question may contribute to how much response you receive. When you ask a question which calls for a student to talk about his or her own life, they may be reluctant to answer. This reluctance may come from a fear of revealing something personal about themselves or setting themselves up to be laughed at. Here is a technique that has been successful for me. Instead of asking the class "Has this ever happened to you?" I generalize the question by asking "Has this ever happened to you or someone you know?" By adding the phrase "someone you know," you allow the students to reply without revealing that the experience may be about them personally. Since we know that one of the maxims kids live by is "Don't embarrass me!" this strategy lowers the risk level of their answer.

There isn't a single technique or one-size-fits-all solution that will result in getting all kids to talk. Each class is different and each student unique. You will have to use a variety of methods as you search for what works for you and your students. Mix and match the suggestions found in this chapter with the other information in this book and the chances are pretty good that you won't have problems with getting kids to talk.

| KEY POINTS |

* ★ Activities give kids something to talk about.

* ★ Barriers to talking must be eliminated.

* ★ Your groups must be psychologically safe places to talk.

* ★ Use both direct and indirect encouragement to get kids to participate.

* ★ No single technique works for all kids.

10 ||| I Don't Know

Three words you don't want to hear during a discussion.

I have been a high school teacher, a prevention specialist, a youth ministry worker, a speaker at youth conferences and a parent. What this really means is that I have had a lot of experience with kids. Let me tell you what I learned from my youngest child, Denise. When she was in her teen years, she would show her burgeoning independence by arguing with me. When she could see herself being verbally backed into a corner, she would start to resort to that age old teenage comeback of "Because." When things really got tough and she couldn't explain her actions any other way, then "Because" always came into use. Of course "Because" doesn't explain anything, but at least to her it sounded like an answer. Then when I pointed out the error of her thinking and there was no way out for her, the last comment by her was always a sarcastic "So." This retort summed up everything that had been said and proved that she was right. What I learned from these frequent exchanges was that when she said "So" it really had a whole lot more meaning behind it than what I was hearing. What I was hearing wasn't always what she was thinking.

I relate this story to you because it brings up a classic situation that can occur in a group discussion. In a discussion it isn't "Because" or "So" that is thrown out hoping for a quick exit from the hot seat, it is "I don't know."

This phrase can kill a discussion faster than any other. It quickly spreads like wildfire throughout the group. As soon as one person invokes the "I don't know" phrase, then it is open season for the rest of the group. Pretty soon you don't have a discussion; it has degenerated into a chorus of "I don't knows." I was helping at a weekend teen retreat as one of the facilitators when this very situation occurred. We had twenty-five junior high aged high-risk girls in attendance and on Friday night a couple of them decided that "I don't know" was going to be their standard answer. In no time every question was met with the same answer from the entire group. However, the "I don't know" comment only works if you allow that reply to be an acceptable answer. Instead of allowing "I don't know" to spread, stop and explore what the student is really trying to say. Other students will then think before they use this simple but revealing comment. We had to stop the retreat and I led a discussion on what "I don't know" really means. Here is a list of what students can mean when they answer "I don't know."

I Don't Know! What your students might really be saying.

- I don't want to share my thoughts with you.

- I haven't thought enough about it yet.

- I'm not sure that my answer makes sense.

- I don't want others to laugh at what I am thinking.

- I don't want to sound like the teacher's pet.

- You've asked a question that calls for me to reveal too much about myself.

- I don't want to sound stupid.

- I want to hear what others say before I give my answer.

- I am having a bad day and "I don't know" is the best I can do right now.

- I wasn't listening and have no idea what you just asked.

- I don't want to put out the energy to think about it right now.

- I don't want to make a fool of myself.

- I want my answer to be perfect before I talk.

- I don't know what answer you're looking for.

- "I don't know" is a safe answer.

- I am hoping the teacher will go on to another student.

- I don't feel safe or accepted in the group.

- I really don't know.

If you are getting a whole string of "I don't knows," then you better see if it is something that you are doing. Try to figure out the real reason behind their answers. Think through my list and see if something there gives you a clue. Be sure that you haven't set them up by not giving them enough information to draw upon, by asking a question that requires them to reveal something very personal, by calling for an opinion too early in the discussion or by asking a question where the answer is too obvious. In previous discussions you may have indicated to the group that there is a specific answer you are looking for. This happens when you go beyond simply acknowledging answers and quantifying them by the remarks you make after certain answers. Examples of this would be remarks such as, "Great answer," "Wonderful," "I really like that answer," etc. See chapter four on "The Teacher's Role During a Discussion" where it talks about using a neutral response for more on this issue.

Here are some responses that I have tried when the "I don't know" answer begins to rear its ugly head.

"What was the first thing that popped into your head when you heard the question?"

"If you did know, what would you say?"

"Pretend you are someone else, what would they say?"

"Make something up!"

"Ask me a question so I can help you understand what I am asking."

The purpose of these questions is to let the student know that just because they say "I don't know" that doesn't get them off the hook. You really are interested in hearing from them and are willing to work hard to get a response. Once the students realize that you will not give up easily, they are less likely to try and use "I don't know" as an easy escape route since it will put them on the spot for an even longer period of time. It becomes easier for the student to just contribute the first time when asked and let the teacher move on.

When all else fails, admit to the group that you realize that their minds just aren't ready for an open discussion. Instead ask for each of them to respond in writing to a couple of your questions.

Writing always seems to loosen up the thought processes. Use some of the techniques mentioned in chapter four on "Discussion Formats" and chapter nine on "Getting Kids To Talk" which can help. With the proper approach, you may never find yourself in this situation.

Another word that can disrupt your discussion is the word "pass." This term is usually associated with the substance abuse treatment/mental health field, but since many of today's students have received these types of services, the practice has found its way into the regular classroom. The word is appropriately used in a treatment setting or during a group therapy session. If the topic or question that is being discussed is a sensitive one to a particular person in the group, they may choose to "pass" when it is their turn to talk. This allows them to gather their thoughts and get their emotions under control before having to address the issue. If you are a counselor, social worker, therapist, etc., then the use of this technique is useful. However, let's examine a classroom or other general setting. The topics you address are not intensely personal. You will be talking with kids about life skills or general life experiences. You should not be asking questions of a personal nature such as their sexual history, alcoholic parents, suicide attempts or personal substance abuse. Therefore students should not have to evoke the term "pass" to control their emotions. If a student begins to disclose information of a personal nature which you feel is too sensitive for general classroom discussion, ask them to hold that thought and meet with them after class to talk about their situation. The problem with allowing students to "pass" during a general classroom discussion is that as soon as you permit one student to do so, the rest will leap in with both feet and soon every question you ask will be met with the answer "pass."

| KEY POINTS |

* "I don't know" is an answer that only works when the teacher lets it.

* These three words can quickly kill a discussion.

* Use probing questions to draw out the student's response.

* The word "pass" can be just as deadly to a discussion as "I don't know."

11 ||| Nuts and Bolts

Practical solutions to everyday problems.

My wife's father, Donald, was a backyard mechanic. On weekends and after his regular job, he would work in the garage fixing his or a friend's car. Sometimes when he would complete a job, there would be a couple of small parts left over. If the repair seemed to work even without these parts, he would declare those extra parts to be "pocket pieces" and the job was done. That's what this chapter is. All of the information that is left over from the other chapters will be gathered here. These are my "pocket pieces." Your discussion would probably work without these nuts and bolts, but with them I know you will succeed!

How do I get my students to calm down after an activity so I can start the discussion? Getting kids to settle down after an activity can be difficult. Here is a technique that I have used with great success. I call it "Transition Time." This is a process that you will teach to the students before you even conduct an activity. After teaching them the process, have them practice it a couple of times so everyone understands what you want them to do. Explain to the students that after finishing an activity you will be calling out the phrase "transition one." You will then take a deep breath and let it out slowly. If any students wish to breath along with you that is fine. If they wish to continue talking quietly, that is fine also. Repeat the same process by calling out "transition two." Once again, any students who want to may breath along with you. However when you call out "transition three," everyone *must* stop talking and take a breath along with you. When you are finished letting this third breath out, the class is to remain quiet and wait for your next instruction. This gets them ready to move into the processing time. If you have a very active class that still has a hard time calming down, add closing their eyes during "transition three." Closing their eyes gives them something else to concentrate on and removes any visual stimulation.

There are a number of other possible techniques you can also use. These include raising your hand when you are ready for the class to become quiet, turning the room lights off and on, counting down verbally from five to one or by simply using your fingers to show the countdown without saying anything, clapping your hands, etc. Any number of methods will work. The key to making it work is to choose a technique that you are comfortable with, teach it to your groups and use it all the time. With repeated use, the class will become familiar with the process and respond accordingly.

How much information about the topic should I give them before the activity? First of all, you need to decide how you are going to use the activity. There are two ways in which to incorporate an activity into your lesson plan. The first is called "discovery." Here you would want to give very little information about the topic and then use the discussion time to allow the students to discover for themselves the meaning of the activity and how it relates to the day's topic. This technique is also known as "back loading" the activity because most of the content of your lesson will take place after the activity has been conducted. The second method is called "reinforcement." Here you teach the entire concept before you do the activity. The activity is then being used as a hands-on means to reinforce what you have already taught them. This technique is called "front loading" the activity because most of the content of your lesson will be given before the activity takes place. Both of these methods serve a purpose. As a general rule, you will want to front load your activity when the group you are working with has very little knowledge concerning the topic you are teaching. For example, if you want to teach anger management skills, the group will need information regarding what anger management is before they can make any meaningful discoveries. This would be an example of front loading. On the other hand, if you have already covered anger management, you might use an activity to help them more fully understand concepts you have already taught or make additional life applications. This is an example of back loading. You will need to decide which method will meet your specific lesson plan.

How do I know when to transition from one phase to the next when using the "What, So What, Now What" outline? Here is a general rule of thumb: Move on when you notice that the answers are becoming repetitious or that the students are starting to disengage. Examples of disengaging behavior would be side conversations starting to take place, eye contact among the group diminishing, students putting their heads down on their desks, etc. When these signs start to appear, you need to reenergize the group either by asking a new question or moving to the next phase. I don't have specific times for you to spend in each section, but I will give you a comparison. I find that the "So What" section takes the longest period of time since the students are expressing their opinions. The "What" section and the "Now What" section are usually about equal. The "What" section doesn't take very long because your purpose is simply to get the discussion off to a good start when you are using these questions. The "Now What" section doesn't take very long because you are only asking one or two questions during this phase. If you use a writing format for the "Now What" section, this will increase the time necessary to complete it.

I personally like to keep a rather brisk and upbeat pace as I move through the discussion steps. This doesn't mean that I short change the discussion, but I do keep it moving. In the large group format I call on students rapidly and throw out a new question as soon as the meat of the question has been covered. When they are in small groups, I give them a specific amount of time to discuss each question. This puts some urgency into the discussion and makes sure the students aren't using the time to just socialize.

How long should I spend discussing? This is like asking "How long should a rope be?" It depends on what you want the rope to do. This is a tough question to give a specific answer to since so much of it depends on the activity that you have conducted, the topic that you are discussing, the amount of previous knowledge regarding the topic the students have, the age and mental development of your group, past experience your group has had with processing and the time your schedule permits.

Let's take a look at these factors. Some activities have a lot of issues that can be discussed and others are trying to get a single point across. If it is a single point activity, don't try to make the discussion time last forever. Let a few questions solidify the point and move on. I am afraid that some people determine the success of a discussion by how long it lasts. They feel that the longer the discussion, the more successful. Not true! Some activities are so clear in what they show that the point is immediately obvious. The same is true with certain topics. If it is a cut-and-dried fact about a certain drug or behavior that you are trying to impress upon your kids, then discuss long enough to make the point and move on. However, some activities can be applied to many different issues. In these cases, decide which issues would be most applicable to your group and cover as many as the group can handle.

Previous knowledge, either that the group brings to the activity or that you explored with them before conducting the activity, has an impact on the processing time. If the students are very familiar with the topic, then more discussion will be generated. If it is a new idea or concept to them, then you will have to take it in shorter time segments and address the topic with multiple activities or lesson plans over a longer period of time. Also, consider the developmental stages of your kids. During different developmental stages they are ready for different approaches to the same concept. As they mature mentally, they will be able to discuss for longer periods of time and, more importantly, with greater complexity.

Past experience or familiarity with the processing process also plays a part. The more experienced your group becomes in sharing opinions and ideas with each other, the longer and more in-depth the discussion time will be. You will have to be patient with them during this learning period.

The last item is the time you have allocated for processing. If you have scheduled ten minutes and it only lasts five, then you need to be sure that you have something else to fill the remaining five minutes rather than trying to fish for five more minutes of discussion time. However, if you have scheduled ten minutes and your time is running out, then you need to be sure that the important parts of the activity have been covered.

I feel that time should not be the deciding factor in determining the length of a discussion. However, when time constraints are an issue, choose your most important questions and concentrate on those. If the kids are still volunteering information, then you should keep the discussion going. Some of the groups most meaningful discoveries will be made after all of the obvious answers have been given. Conversely, if you are pulling teeth to get participation, then you need to either end the discussion or change the line of questions to something that is more relevant and appropriate for your group.

The real answer to the question, "How long?" is that you should end the discussion when you feel your teaching objective has been taught. If you end the discussion before you have reached this point, then conducting the activity was not a wise use of your time since the purpose of doing the activity was to create a teaching opportunity or a teachable moment. Once you have accomplished your teaching objective, any further time spent in discussion is using up valuable class time that could be spent doing something else. How long should you discuss? As long as it takes and no longer.

When the students are in small groups, how do I get them to stop talking so I can move on? First of all, state how much time the group has to answer the question you have asked and then be sure you keep them informed of how much time they have left to talk. Give them a five or ten second warning before you are going to end the discussion time for that question.

How can I get the entire class quiet when they are in separate parts of the room discussing? I have two methods to get a large group quiet. I use these whether I am conducting the activity or in the discussion phase. The first method I call "quiet with dignity." When I want them to stop talking I raise my hand. Anyone who sees me raise my hand should raise their hand. This is the signal to finish your sentence and then be quiet. I can quiet a room in about fifteen seconds. The second method is called a "freeze command." I use this method when I want their attention immediately. I will call out the words "peanut butter" and anyone that hears me will repeat back the word "jelly." When you hear the word jelly, everyone immediately stops talking and turns towards me for further instructions. While conducting an activity, I use the freeze command when I see behavior taking place that is not safe or grossly inappropriate. I also use it during a discussion to get their attention when I realize that they need further clarification about a question I gave them or I want to give them a short follow-up question.

What about really young children? Until kids reach the age of about seven, they really don't have the mental maturity to do much abstract thinking. I would recommend that you ask children in grades K-2 the "What" questions and then just tell them the answers to the "So What" and "Now What" questions. Once again, this of course depends on the maturity of the group you are dealing with. You can tell if your students are benefiting from the discussion.

How do I get my students into groups for discussion? You shouldn't be too cute with this. Using games or other time consuming methods to get them into small groups will cut into the discussion time. Your first option is to use the same groups for discussion that they were in during the activity. If that doesn't meet your needs, then look to other options. Be sure that you move them into their discussion groups before you give out any further instructions or ask any questions. Kids are very social by nature and will want to be sure that they have secured a place in a group. Therefore, if you say that you want them in groups of five, they will stop listening to anything else you say until they have found a group. If you don't put them in groups first, you will find your-self repeating your instructions over and over again.

I use a number of ways to get them into groups. You can just assign groups of five or have them count off by fives and then have the ones be a group, the twos are a group, etc. You may get the question "Can I change groups?" This question can ruin the discussion time. It changes the focus from what is going to be discussed to who everyone is with. I always answer this question the same. My reply is "No and please never ask again." This lets the students know that I do not change students around and that they are wasting their time asking me. There are only two reasons kids want to change groups. The first reason is that they don't like the people they are with and the second is that they like some other people better. Neither one of these reasons are important ones to me. If for some reason you want to separate certain people or have specific people together, then plan ahead for this and already have your groups determined and written down ahead of time.

Another time saving method is to have predetermined groups. For example, let's say you want to have three different variations of groups with four people in them. Call one variation the orange plan. Make a large wall poster that has as many four people groupings as you need to accommodate everyone in your class and that becomes the orange plan. Designate another variation as the purple plan. Once again make up groups of four people moving your students around so they aren't with the same people. Continue to make group designations until you have the number of variations you want. Now when you need groups of four, you can just indicate to the students which color plan you are using and they will move to those groups. This will give you a way to move them into groups quickly. These groups can be changed periodically. Here is an example of this method using two group variations with a class of twelve students.

ORANGE PLAN

Don, Sally, Malcom, Jerry

Shelly, Jesse, Michael, Jose

Terran, Kelly, Chris, John

PURPLE PLAN

Sally, Jerry, Jesse, John

Don, Kelly, Shelly, Jose

Malcom, Michael,

Chris, Terran

How large should discussion groups be? The question isn't really how large the group is, but how many kids are engaged in the discussion. You may be having a great large group discussion with everyone raising their hands and listening to each other's comments or you might have two person discussion pairs with no one talking. So numbers alone shouldn't determine the size of the discussion groups. With that said, here are some guidelines. If you use partners when discussing, it is hard for someone to hide. I know that every student is either talking to someone or listening to someone. When dividing into small groups, I generally avoid forming trios because two of the students are often more compatible with one another which leaves one student feeling left out. Groups larger than four or five can lead to some members of the group becoming very passive and letting the others do all of the talking.

How can I hold students accountable for what they have learned during an activity? Grades, participation and accountability are all buzz words that are found in today's educational climate. When some people hear the word activity, they immediately think of games. Activities are different than games. They have a teaching objective rather than just being fun. To measure how well each student has grasped the objective you had in mind, you can utilize a number of the various discussion formats that are described in chapter four. Particular notice should be paid to the formats titled Buzz Groups, Written Answers, and Anonymous

Comments. All of these formats require some form of written documentation. Choose a couple of the more important questions from your discussion and have the students turn in their answers to those questions in written form. You may then use what they turn in for your grading needs. You may use the answers that they have written while the discussion took place or you can finish the group discussion and then assign the work to be graded as an additional assignment to be completed during the class period or as homework. I would suggest that you keep a file of some of the students' most insightful written comments. These can then be used to show other educators or parents who might question whether the activities you use are beneficial.

| KEY POINTS |

* Transition time is a procedure that can be used to quiet the class after an activity.

* Give a lot of information before the activity if you are using the activity to reinforce what they have learned.

* Give very little information before the activity if you want the students to discover for themselves the object of the lesson.

* Don't spend any more time in discussion than it takes to reach your teaching objective.

* Getting kids into groups for discussion should be done as quickly as possible to allow more time for the actual discussion.

* If student accountability is an issue, have important discussion questions answered in writing and then grade them.

12 ||| Suggestions from the Front Lines

Learn from the successes of others.

I feel that one way we can help the kids we work with is to share our own experiences with others in the field. Therefore, I put out a call to other professionals who lead discussions to send in their tips and hints concerning how to lead a discussion. This chapter contains their responses. You may read suggestions that contradict each other. But that is the great thing about leading a discussion; there are many different techniques that will bring the desired results. Some of the responses have been edited for length. My personal thanks goes out to each person who took the time to send in their comments. The information I have listed for each of them was current at the time I received their response. If you have anything to contribute, please feel free to send me an e-mail at staff@activelearning.org. I will be able to share your comments via my newsletter which is found at the web site www.activelearning.org

Tauna Larson, Educational Talent Search counselor, Monticello, Utah

Let your kids know that after every activity a discussion will be held. Ask questions that are appropriate for the students you work with. Don't use a lot of questions and don't read the questions. Start off the discussion and then LISTEN to the students. Have several different roads the discussion could take. Encourage all to have a say.

Al Montgomery, retired high school principal, Metaire, Louisiana

A teacher has to have good management skills for the discussion to be meaningful. Be prepared to "bring in" students who don't participate, make sure everyone gets to speak, don't permit talk "hogs" and be ready to use different examples to explain concepts not understood. Discussions are easier to manage, and more inclusive, when desks are arranged in a circle or two row circle.

Guy Beard, Peer Helping & Psychology teacher, Pensacola, Florida

Avoid prejudicing the group with your own understandings or interpretations of the activity. Often when attempting to stimulate a discussion, we make "suggestions" that end up shifting the discussion in the direction we want it to go; instead give students as much freedom as possible to arrive at their own understanding.

Kara Dodds, 5th-6th grade multi-age teacher, Salt Lake City, Utah

Involve all of the students. Don't just call on those raising their hands. The more discussions you have as a class, the less apprehensive students will be to talk. Through having frequent discussions, you will create an atmosphere where the students feel comfortable enough to share. If during the discussion a student should go a little off from the topic, let them. So many students do not get the opportunity to talk with parents at home and it is important for educators to allow them to discuss what is on their mind. Chances are that if a question or concern is on one student's mind, it is on the minds of several others.

Janan Szurek, school social worker, Montgomery, Illinois

Always allow enough time for processing. There is no purpose in doing the activity without processing. Ask questions that will guide the students to the answers that meet your teaching objective. The key—guidance. Do not tell the students what you are looking for. By guiding them to the answers, they become empowered and they tend to retain more information. As you discuss and process the activity, write important points on the board and have students take notes in their notebooks. This creates another modality for learning.

Holly Wamsley, Mathematics teacher, West Valley City, Utah

Be patient and flexible. Sometimes your discussion takes a totally different turn than intended but is equally as valuable. Keep trying. Practice makes perfect. Also listen. You learn a great deal about your students if you learn to listen to their responses and not just funnel the discussion the direction you wanted it to go.

Shirlie Freytag, Guidance counselor grades 5-8, Wray, Colorado

One of the most effective questions I have begun using with my 7th and 8th graders is "What do you think I wanted you to get out of this activity?" Obviously I couldn't use this the first time I did an activity, but I have found that the kids feel empowered when they are given control of the conversation by starting out with this less directive questioning. Ninety-nine percent of the time they are right on target regarding where I was headed, but often they include more than I was trying to get, which expands the discussion. Another advantage is that it tends to cut very quickly to the heart of the matter, making use of time more effective.

Listen for what is unsaid as well as what is said. As a counselor involved in guidance lessons, I use lots of activities because I have found them invaluable in opening up discussions with troubled kids in a private setting afterward. Often the activity was the catalyst for feeling safe enough to approach related (and even unrelated) issues.

Most importantly, be sure you're not doing most of the talking.

Ruth Gillmore, Health and Peer Assistance Program, Temple City, California

Prior to the activity, make certain that you know where you want to go with the activity. What key points do you want the students to go away with? I use post-its just in case I should forget. Be patient after asking the students for their thoughts and opinions. Don't think because there is a pause that nothing is happening. Processing takes a long time for some kids. I've found that sometimes they are not quite sure of how to react or respond because they have never had information presented to them in such a direct way where they have been a part of the learning process. Sometimes, restating the question helps too.

Laurel A. Avery-DeToy, lead teacher-mentor in health education, Rochester, New York

Discussion is tough for many new teachers. They are so eager to have student response, they often answer their own questions before the kids have a chance to process. I have encouraged my new teachers to relax and give them five seconds to think and process. I have also encouraged higher level thinking skills, getting away from yes/no responses. This is really important, as I have found that sometimes the obvious answer isn't always what they get and then I learn too!

Angie Gerdes, high school teacher, Leander, Texas

Have students journal or write responses on paper to get them to wind down after activities. Sometimes students are hyped up after the activities and it's hard to get them to sit still in a group and discuss. Writing some responses down will help students calm down a bit. Then they can share their responses with the class.

Craig Rasmussen, principal of an alternative high school, Ephraim, Utah

I select the questions that I would like to use ahead of time and may eliminate some in the process if the discussion of one question has touched on the topic of another question. Don't stick to the order or content of the questions unswervingly. If one question opens up a vigorous discussion on something the kids are interested in, seize the moment.

Randy Jo Nielsen, therapist, Fort Smith, Arkansas

Don't help out too quickly.

Ann Banfield, Health Education, Naperville, Illinois

Do not let one student capitalize the floor. This student will "scare" others off, or make them feel like they are "off the hook" with having to speak. Draw students in by asking for their personal reactions or thoughts. Also, realize that a discussion does not need to last the whole period to be meaningful. Some of the most wonderful discussions in my classroom have taken place in ten minutes.

Lisa M. Silmser, English teacher, Anoka, Minnesota

Here are a couple of discussion formats that have worked well for me when helping my students process an activity.

Hat Discussion: After an activity, I will have the kids take strips of paper and quickly write down responses to a series of questions. They must write neatly, but don't have to be too elaborate. When I have asked all of the questions and the kids have responded in writing, they put their slips in a hat. Then without reading the questions again, one person at a time will draw a slip, read the written comment aloud and respond to it. We never get to all of the slips, but we usually cover most of the questions. This also helps every kid process because the less verbal kids have a chance to think a bit before the discussion really gets going.

Paired Discussion: I divide the kids into pairs, using notecards, birthdays, height or some other goofy reason. Then I ask the questions and the kids discuss in pairs before coming to the large group. This also helps the kids who tend to be more shy get involved. They are more likely to share with the large group after this kind of start.

Some of the best discussions I have had have come from secondary questioning. I always ask "Why do you think that?" This pushes kids to avoid pat answers and move to providing background for their opinions or feelings. Middle school kids are too quick to give the answer that first comes to their minds. After asking why so often, my students begin to automatically respond with "I think that because . . ." before I can even get the "why" out. The other cool thing that has happened is that kids will then push for "why" from each other—they learn not to settle for unsupported statements.

Another technique I use is walking the students back through an activity before opening up the discussion. When we do a more complicated, multi-step activity, I will have the kids take a minute afterward and sit quietly with their eyes closed. I will then talk them through the steps of the activity again and include questions that will prompt them to visualize the activity. This allows kids who only focus on the event to slow down and consider how they felt during the activity. Many kids are moving too quickly during the activity to realize that they were thinking or feeling anything.

Linda Johnston, 6th grade math teacher, Apple Valley, Minnesota

I have used the "What . . . So What . . . Now What" to prepare for teachable moments. An example . . . several students didn't do well on a test. To present my concerns and disappointments I prepared my speech on a transparency to share my "What" (there were several scores lower than what their abilities were) "So What" (grades were lowered, test corrections needed to be done) and "Now What" (goal setting for the future). This outline can be used to present many topics/areas of discussion . . . America attacked . . . "What" (the towers were hit and collapsed, many good people died) . . . "So What" (could share feelings, how it affects us) . . . "Now What" (what America is doing . . . what we as individuals can do to stay strong, united, believing).

Barbara Sunley, Family and Consumer Sciences teacher, Wamego, Kansas

I look for ways to apply each activity to what I'm currently teaching in class at the time. For example, when I teach Preschool (that's a high school FACS class that teaches students how to run a preschool), I ask the class after the activity called "Chain Gang" (from the book **More Activities That Teach**) what kind of implications they could draw from the activity? They of course came up with the idea about cooperation and teamwork—which is important to preschool teachers. When they talked about frustrations, I was able to point out to them that certain activities they plan for the children will be frustrating to the children too because of their developmental stages.

Maggi Straley, 6th Grade Guidance counselor, Logan, Utah

Before the activity, write on the whiteboard or on a large sheet of paper at the front of the room one or two "Now What" questions. At the end of the activity, have students pair up if they aren't already in pairs for the activity. Decide who will go first (the tallest, the longest hair, etc.). Instruct the kids to pick one or both of the questions from the board to answer with their partner. With a stopwatch or timer, give person #1 sixty seconds to give his or her answer to the question. Person #2 only listens, no comments, arguments or comebacks. If person #1 finishes before the sixty seconds is up, then he or she can talk about the other question. Then they trade roles for the next sixty seconds. This seems to help the students loosen up a little and at the same time gets them thinking about their ideas about the activity and prepares them to participate in the group discussion that follows. They can practice expressing their ideas about the activity with only one other person listening.

Lisa Miller, Family and Consumer Sciences teacher, Vermilion, Ohio

To help get kids to talk, I give each student a number as they walk into class and tell them they will use it in a later activity. After the activity is over, then call the numbers randomly to have students answer questions concerning the activity. I have also used this method to grade students as to whether or not they were paying attention during the activity, depending on their answer. This method is great for block scheduling at the high school level where you need to take grades every day.

When I know the activity will take most of the class and we will not be able to discuss it right away, I will type up questions and have the students answer them for homework. The students get points for returning their homework and then we have a class discussion. This helps the discussion run smoothly because the students have the answers in front of them and they are more willing to share.

Before an activity be careful not to give too much away by explaining the "plot" before you actually do the activity. It is also helpful to make a list of everything you will need for an activity and then store it in a large zip lock bag for next year, so it is there when you need it.

Doris Smith, High School Health teacher and Curriculum coordinator, Clayton, Missouri

I find if I have some strong personalities in the class, we tend to get "group think," where one person talks and we all just agree. In these situations I often have my students journal in response to discussion questions and then discuss. It seems that if they think about and write about their own thoughts on a topic they are more likely to verbalize them and not go along with the crowd.

Sydney Sauer, Elementary School counselor, Kansas City, Missouri

With young students I usually pose an initial processing question such as "I am wondering what you think some 4th graders might think about _____ (i.e. peer pressure, fears, smoking, etc.)? Your answer doesn't have to necessarily be what you think, but what you might have heard others say." This seems to let kids feel safe about sharing ideas when I phrase it in that way. It is a good practice to think about the questions you will ask before you conduct the activity.

13 |||| A Discussion Checklist

Plan your discussion one step at a time.

A successful discussion requires a certain amount of planning. In my first book, **Activities That Teach**, I have an activity where students compete to build the tallest tower using marshmallows and toothpicks (titled Marshmallow Tower). Unfortunately, most of the towers fall over before the activity is completed because in the students' haste to make them tall, they forgot to give the tower a large enough foundation. This same failure can occur when leading a discussion. Sometimes we are so excited to begin talking that we forget to properly prepare. Here is a list of some of the things that you should consider as you get ready to lead a discussion. Each item may not apply to every discussion, but the list will give you a place to begin your planning. If you need further information regarding any of the items, the page number where that information will be found is listed.

1. How much time have you allotted in your lesson plan for discussion? Page 7

2. What is your primary teaching objective for the activity? Page 12

3. Which questions will you ask during the "What" step? Page 14

4. Which questions will you ask during the "So What" step? Page 15

5. Which questions will you ask during the "Now What" step? Page 16

6. What points would you like to emphasize during the summarizing step? Page 18

7. Have you explained the four step discussion outline to your students? Page 21

8. Which discussion format will you utilize for each of the first three discussion steps? Page 26

9. How can your room be arranged to best allow for easy student-to-student discussion? Page 41

10. Where will you be positioned during the discussion? Page 42

11. Have you followed the guidelines for good questions?Page 47

12. Are you going to use a written list of questions? Page 55

13. What follow-up questions will you use to keep the discussion from stalling? Page 56

14. How will you end the discussion? Page 58

15. How comfortable are you with silence during a discussion? Page 63

16. Do you usually use neutral responses after student comments? Page 64

17. Do you use a variety of discussion formats? Page 67

18. Do you give a time warning before students are to end their small group discussions? Page 67

19. Do you talk too much during the discussion? Page 68

20. Do you control how much personal information is revealed by students during a discussion? Page 68

21. Have you discussed with your class guidelines for student behavior during a discussion? Page 73

22. Is your classroom psychologically safe during a discussion? Page 83

23. Do you encourage students, both directly and indirectly, to participate in the discussion? Page 84

24. Have you considered which techniques you might use to draw out timid or hesitant students? Page 85

25. Is your class having a problem with the "I don't know" syndrome? Page 91

26. Have you practiced a procedure with your kids to get the class ready for the discussion after an activity? Page 97

27. How much information are you going to give the students before you conduct the activity and how much will you give them after conducting the activity? Page 98

28. How will you determine when the discussion should be ended? Page 100

29. How will you move the students into small groups when needed? Page 103

30. If necessary, how will you give students a grade for the class period when you have conducted an activity? Page 105

14 |||| You Can Do It!

I realize that fun isn't always educational and education isn't always fun, but when the two come together—it just doesn't get any better.

One definition of the word "conduct" as defined by Webster's New World Dictionary is "The process or way of managing or directing, to lead or to guide." The word "conduct" is the root from which the word "conductor" came. The leader of a discussion has the same responsibility as the conductor of an orchestra. Just as the orchestra conductor must deal with the musical arrangement, the position of the musical instruments, the speed and volume of the piece and musicians themselves, you as the discussion leader have similar variables to contend with. The discussion leader must decide upon the appropriate discussion format, choose the questions to be asked, settle upon the arrangement of the room, control the flow and speed of the discussion and, of course deal with the students themselves. One big difference between the two events is that the resulting outcome of a successful concert is a pleasing musical presentation, while the outcome of a well planned and successful discussion is the personal growth of the kids you work with.

Every group is different and their needs unique. As the person who best understands those needs, you will be the one responsible for putting together the various ingredients that are required to make a successful discussion. This book has given you the information you need to make a difference in the lives of kids. Don't worry about how skilled you are or if you have enough experience to conduct a successful discussion. Realize that hands-on learning also applies to you. The best way to learn how to lead a discussion is to lead one. In chapter one I gave you two basic rules that were to guide you throughout this book: **"Use what works for you and change what doesn't"** and **"Both you and your students will get better the more times you use active learning."** Always remember to keep these rules in mind.

One last word of advice—have fun with your groups! If you are having a good time during the discussion, then the chances are your students are also having a good time. Take the information in this book, modify it to meet your situation, and in the words of a famous advertising campaign—Just Do It!

OTHER BOOKS BY TOM JACKSON

Sample activities may be viewed at www.activelearning.org

Don't miss out! Be sure you have all of Tom's powerful, hands-on activities and discussion techniques which you can use immediately to make a real difference in the lives of kids. Each book has different activities in them.

These activities and discussion strategies will create excitement and increased learning anywhere there is a group of kids. Thousands of professionals have successfully used these activities with elementary and secondary groups and have found them effective with inner city, suburban, rural, high-risk and at-risk populations. These fun, hands-on activities have been tested in the real world of classrooms, after school programs, churches, prevention programs, treatment centers, juvenile detention centers, etc.

Students learn best by doing! All of Tom's activity books contain user-friendly activities that get kids involved in their own learning process and let them have fun at the same time. The books include opening chapters on how-to use activities and tips for leading effective discussions. Each activity is followed by a list of questions that can be used to help you transfer what you did during the activity to real life applications. These activities can be used in classrooms, counseling and support groups, youth programs, after school programs, churches or anywhere else you would find a group of kids. Great for all grade levels!

Activities That Teach: 60 hands-on activities that address topics such as alcohol, tobacco and drug prevention, and which teach skills related to communication, values, working together, problem solving, stress management, goal setting, self-esteem, decision making and more.

234 pages. Retail price: $15.95 (Case discounts available)

More Activities That Teach: All different activities than Tom's first book. 82 additional hands-on activities that address topics such as alcohol, tobacco and drug prevention, and which teach skills related to anger management, resisting peer pressure, diversity, violence and gang prevention, communication, values, working together, problem solving, stress management, goal setting, self-esteem, decision making and more.

341 pages. Retail price: $18.95 (Case discounts available)

Activities That Teach Family Values: 52 new activities that can be used by parents, character education programs, small group sessions, church groups or after-school programs to help adults stop preaching to kids and start sharing with them instead. Once again Tom's hands-

on approach is used to address topics such as caring, cooperation, honesty, perseverance, respect, responsibility, service to others and much, much more.

Retail price: $14.95 (Case discounts available)

Still More Activities That Teach: 55 all new activities which address all of the topics from previous books, along with these new topics: conflict resolution, respect, responsibility, school-to-careers, team building, media influence and healthy lifestyles. Discussion questions at the end of each activity are divided into easy-to-use categories.

257 pages. Retail price $15.95 (Case discounts available)

For ordering information about any of Tom's books:

Call toll free (888) 588-7078

between the hours of 7:00 a.m. and 7:00 p.m. Mountain Time

Write: Active Learning Center, 3835 West 800 North, Cedar City UT 84720

FAX: 435-586-0185

web site: www.activelearning.org

e-mail: staff@activelearning.org

Mastercard, Visa, Checks, or Purchase Orders gladly accepted

Invite Tom Jackson
to Speak at Your Conference, School or
Organization

That's right! Wouldn't it be great to have Tom come to your conference or school and share with you his creative, yet practical hands-on activities? Tom's activities have been described by teachers and others who work with children and youth as "Simply the best life skill activities I have ever used! They teach life skills in such a way that kids not only learn, but love doing them." Or you can broaden the topic by having Tom talk about active learning as a teaching tool which can energize any classroom or program. The length of Tom's presentations can be tailored to meet your needs.

Reading about the activities is exciting, but there is no substitute for experiencing them. Tom uses his "learn by doing" approach to walk you through a number of activities from his books. Here is a chance to ask questions, get insider tips and learn first hand how to process and discuss the activities with your kids. Hundreds of teachers, counselors, youth workers and others have participated in Tom's workshops, and one of the most common remarks is, "I wish we had more time. This is the most useful workshop I have ever attended."

Tom is available for keynote presentations, conference breakouts, workshops, teacher in-services, etc. Funding sources that have been used successfully by other organizations include staff development, Safe and Drug Free Schools, Title I, At-Risk and High Risk, as well as special grants and community resources. Join up with a neighboring school, school district or organization and save money by sharing travel costs when Tom stays more than one day in your part of the country. We will even try to book another workshop in your area to help you save money on travel if you will give us other likely people to contact!

Give Janet Jackson a call toll free at (888) 588-7078 between 7:00 a.m. and 7:00 p.m. Mountain Time and ask for Tom's speaker packet. Or, just call Janet and suggest to her a person in your school district or organization who would be interested in hearing more about Tom and she'll contact them directly.

Hear Tom Jackson on Leading a Discussion

Activities are powerful tools when the group leader has the skills needed to lead a meaningful discussion. The best way to learn about leading a discussion is from someone who knows the subject. That person is Tom Jackson. He has worked with kids in all types of situations and has led thousands of discussions. Forget about learning through trial and error—let Tom show you the ins and outs of leading a successful discussion.

Tom's presentation can be given as a keynote address, a conference breakout, a half day workshop or an all day training. Discover which discussion techniques work with kids and which ones don't. If your group is new to processing, then Tom can give them the tools they need to conduct a successful discussion. If your group are old hands at leading discussions, then Tom will help them sharpen their techniques and give them additional strategies.

For scheduling information or to receive a speaker's packet call Janet Jackson toll free at (888) 588-7078 between 7:00 a.m. and 7:00 p.m. Mountain Time. You may also find information at the web site www.activelearning.org

Combine Activities and Discussion into a 2-Day Workshop!

Have Tom Jackson for two days and get the best of both worlds. Your group will experience a variety of activities, learn how to conduct an activity and discover techniques that make the discussion after the activity meaningful and educational. This is a practical, hands-on workshop that will equip the attendees to conduct activities and lead the following discussion. When the two days are over, the participants will be ready to use a variety of active learning methods with the kids they work with.

For scheduling information or to receive a speaker's packet call Janet Jackson toll free at (888) 588-7078 between 7:00 a.m. and 7:00 p.m. Mountain Time. You may also find information at the web site www.activelearning.org

Parents, Parenting Instructors, Parent/School Organizations and Others Who Are Interested in Helping Families

Help families help themselves! Invite Tom Jackson to make a presentation to the parents in your area. Tom doesn't conduct the usual parenting workshop where someone tells parents how they should parent. Instead, he gives parents easy to do, hands-on activities that can be done right in their own homes to open up the lines of communication and discuss important topics with their children in a non-threatening way. Tom also conducts workshops specifically for parenting instructors which focus on how to facilitate parent trainings using Tom's activities.

Explore the values of caring, cooperation, honesty, perseverance, respect, responsibility, and service to others along with other topics. Rather than telling you what to believe, the activities provide a user-friendly vehicle to allow each parent the opportunity to share their own values with their children and have fun at the same time.

Reading about an activity is exciting, but there is no substitute for experiencing them. Tom uses his "learn by doing" approach to let you participate in a number of activities from his book **Activities That Teach Family Values.** Here is a chance to ask questions, get insider tips and learn first hand how to use the activities to discuss values with your kids.

Tom is available for keynote presentations, conference breakouts, workshops and evening presentations. These can be done for parents, trainers of parents or others who work with families. Another option is to conduct a workshop for parents and their children ages 7 to 15½. Have them actually experience the activities together and see how much fun they really are!

Give Janet Jackson a call toll free at (888) 588-7078 between 7:00 a.m. and 7:00 p.m. Mountain Time and ask for Tom's speaker packet. Or, just give Janet a call and suggest to her a person in your school district or organization who would be interested in hearing more about Tom and she'll contact them directly.

Visit the Active Learning Foundation's Web Site
www.activelearning.org
The Active Learning Foundation is a non-profit corporation that is dedicated to helping individuals, families, organizations and communities help themselves through education and skill building. Tom Jackson is the founder and

director of the Foundation. Here is a brief summary of what you will find there.

Speaking Information: Check here if you are considering having Tom Jackson come do a workshop for your group or present at a conference. You will find his vita, costs, travel needs and letters of recommendation along with descriptions of the various topics that he addresses.

Activity Books: Each of Tom's activity books are described along with pricing and ordering information. Also available are the covers of each book and some sample activities.

Teacher's Corner: Check out some activities and research that might be useful.

Parent's Corner: See what activities and research might be helpful for you to use within your own family or as part of a parent training program.

Overheads: Read all of the quotes that Tom uses in his presentations.

Funny One Liners: Nothing here but fun stuff.

Newsletter: Here you will find the latest research concerning how kids learn and active learning. You will also find information concerning workshops, new books and other resource information.

Real Life Stories: People who work with children and youth have shared their success stories regarding active learning.